Contemporary
AMERICAN SCULPTURE

Contemporary

AMERICAN SCULPTURE

C. LUDWIG BRUMMÉ

Foreword by WILLIAM ZORACH

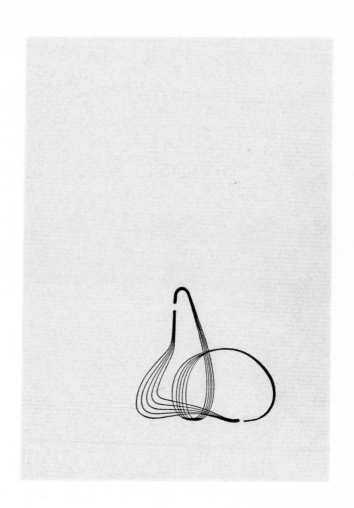

CROWN PUBLISHERS
New York

This book is dedicated to
Seymour Hacker through
whose faith and effort it
reached the light of day.

Contents

INTRODUCTION
by William Zorach

ENVIRONMENT and national influences have played a major part in the development of art in the past. Today, in art, we are truly one world and the art heritage of all ages and all nations is part of all of us. New ideas and new approaches spread like a conflagration over the whole art world. Some of these ideas are vital and meaningful; others are exciting and momentary. There are no isolationists in art. We may reject certain ideas and embrace others but it is natural sympathy and selection that determine our direction, not ignorance or unawareness. The quality of a work of art of any time and any place — whether fundamentally creative or the development of a creative tendency — lies in the artist, himself; in his stature as an artist and a human being, and in his power of putting into a work of art the innate quality of life — his sensitivity, his comprehension, and his creative vision.

Ludwig Brummé has compiled a book of sculpture today, here in these United States, not just for the student of sculpture, but for the people of this country, that they may know their sculptors and be enriched by the living and cultural value of their work. Sculpture should be as much a part of daily life as literature and music. Creating sculpture is one thing, seeing it is another. The sculptor must have vision to create, the person who would enjoy sculpture must have vision to see. To absorb the true meaning of sculpture and derive real pleasure from it, we must look at it with open eyes and open minds.

To appreciate one must not only look but see; one must not only respond with the mind but with the heart. One must approach sculpture with an open mind and let it speak in its own language. Even with an open mind a piece of sculpture either appeals to one or does not. Too great an effort to see and understand defeats itself. One must not stand in awe trying to trace a resemblance to known forms which may never have been intended; or try to read into it meanings which the sculptor may never have had in mind or expressed in form. If one clears one's mind of preconceived ideas — ignoring, at first, what does not appeal — and looks at the sculpture in a receptive and humble spirit, eventually, if anything is there, the beauty of form, the design, the interplay of mass and movement, or the human and emotional content will reveal itself to him. The spirit will be enriched by enjoyment and understanding.

It is not necessary to know the mechanics of sculpture — how structure, form, volume, and rhythm are achieved. It would probably be very enlightening to watch a piece of sculpture in progress — just as sitting through an orchestral rehearsal is very educational to many of us who have little idea of how music is handled and interpreted. All this is very educational if feasible, but emotional and visual enjoyment can be realized by simply looking at works of art in a receptive spirit. A little knowledge sometimes may be a detriment but, if one knows too much of the mechanics of production, it may interfere with his pleasure and true response by involving intellectual processes to the exclusion of art appreciation.

There are those who look at the work of a young artist and say, "Picasso — Brancusi — obviously he admires Lipchitz — he has been looking too hard at Moore"; and having pigeonholed the artist and traced the influence, their self-esteem rises and they feel very smug and superior. This is not an intelligent approach. The world is full of influences, ancient and modern. They are the background of all art and our heritage of development. The only thing to consider is the innate quality of the work of art and the accomplishment of the artist.

Brummé has presented in this book all directions and schools of thought in sculpture, in this way giving an over-all picture of what is happening today, and providing a comprehensive group exhibit. The reader is left free to find his way among the selections to make his own choices; to balance one sculptor against another; to enjoy, hate, resent, and understand. To comprehend the stature of a man, a book on his work alone or a one-man exhibition of his work is necessary; but to understand the breadth and vitality of sculpture today, a book such as this is a necessity. Here we find the accepted and the unaccepted and everything in between.

The most interesting and the most vital characteristic quality in sculpture today is its modern aspect. This aspect could be defined as a highly simplified treatment of forms derived from the visual world, or highly simplified forms conceived without any reference to natural objects. In contrast to this simplification there are the development of very complicated and involved combinations of form, the use of new materials, and an effort to expand sculptural expression beyond the accepted limits of the art. There are also prevalent "constructions" — some related to sculpture in the accepted sense, others by the farthest stretch of the imagination, and still others that have no sculptural significance but are related to architectural problems, applied design, and display. They are products of the ingenuity and versatility of the human brain.

There is no intent on my part to condemn traditional sculpture or to praise superficial and tricky modern sculpture. Fine sculpture is great no matter what form is used or in what age it is created. Quality, expression and taste are continually uppermost in my mind. It is not classical sculpture but the more recent and startling developments that will be disturbing and incomprehensible to the reader.

This is a lively and creative age in sculpture. The overemphasis on shock and novelty is confusing, but shock treatment is beneficial for those firmly established in mental ruts — the only way they can be made aware that life is teeming and vigorous around them. Novelty and ingenuity are at least always intriguing and entertaining. We can enjoy entertainment along with the more serious aspects of sculpture.

There are many tendencies and directions today.

There are those who are enamored of the first enthusiasm captured in the rough sketch; breathing life, promising everything — but only promising. With the "do not touch it — go no farther or you will spoil it" way of working, the artist stops right there with the rough tentative groping for expression and casts it in bronze. This can result in freshness and vitality or it can be a means of avoiding problems — never bringing the

9

idea to its culmination but being satisfied with an easy and superficial result.

There are those who discard craftsmanship, reducing technique to its crudest and most clumsy expression — striving in this way for power and a completely direct contact with their creation.

There are those who make a fetish of technique, busying themselves with surfaces and technical relationships until the work becomes disembodied and sterile. They nullify the living quality of enthusiasm which is so difficult to capture. Yet these works can be highly ornamental and of great use in architecture and industrial design.

There are those who use highly simplified forms and smooth polished surfaces, seeking to refine expression into a pure flame. The dividing line between this concentrated power of expression and an expressionless void is a very subtle one.

One group of sculptors uses exuberant vinelike forms like jungle growth — or expanding globular masses. Some of this is a natural reaction to the phase of sculpture that uses simplified cubistic and polished forms and planes; and again it is related to an appreciation of plant forms, lavish and many-faceted aspects of natural growth, and to the similarity of plant growth to architecture, and even machinery. The basic laws underlying all structural forms have a very distinct family resemblance. The human body, the machine, the flower, the tree, the temple, the bridge, the skyscraper are all based upon the cosmic laws of balance, stress and strains, volumes, vacuums, weights, and solids. This might be called the cosmic pattern of growth. It may be contained in the sphere of the apple or the smooth oval of the fish or it may be as wild and overpowering as the rank growth of the jungle, surviving by mere weight, or by tough cords choking opposition and gaining uncontrolled expansion in every possible form and direction.

Others find expression in jagged and rough forms like the crystalline construction of quartz, the texture and suggestive forms of rocks and powerful mountain masses.

Others use geometrically based planes and solids. These geometric planes effect sweeping rhythms and consecutive movements in space. Sometimes these planes and shapes are painted in colors and serve a very effective purpose in architecture, design, and interior decoration.

There is a school of thought that uses convex and concave forms and surfaces. There are sculptors who deal with holes and vacuums as well as solids — often arbitrarily perforating the forms and surfaces of sculpture — related perhaps to the use of holes in Pre-Columbian sculpture and to the realization that in natural forms which have evolved through time, holes as well as solids are found. Much of this sculpture has real significance in that it stresses the importance of imaginary form and space not there — but supposedly created by the displacements and stresses of form there. These works stimulate the imagination — very much as Leonardo said to his students, "Look for your lines of composition in the disintegrated surfaces of old walls, in the figures seen in the glowing coals and in the constellations of the heavens." Today the sculptor sometimes looks for his lines of inspiration in the suggestions of animals, figures, and abstract forms found in driftwood and in the shapes and textures of stones.

This interest in fantasy and in the texture, shape, and color of stones

10

can become an acceptance of the objects themselves as art — the artist limiting his creative ability to seeing and selecting without contributing. It is very pleasant to stroll along the beach and find stones beautiful in color and form, to pick up driftwood that stirs the imagination. The result might be an exhibition of fascinating objects, but sculpturally it would be the equivalent of an exhibition of blank canvases of various shapes and sizes. A cult developed in Japan where stones became so highly prized for their esoteric value that great prices were set upon them. Not too long ago in England and this country great value was placed on sea shells. The collector can create his illusion about any item and this interest, in time, spills over into the art world.

Modernism is a healthy influence, a revaluation of eternal and fundamental values as well as an adventure into the unknown and a daring that refuses to accept the impossible. Some people accept modernism of any kind without any question just as others accept the academic without a question. Neither is a sound, intelligent approach to art. In looking at an abstract piece of sculpture the important thing is to respond to what is expressed by that piece of sculpture, then to find interest and pleasure in the means used to accomplish this. Look for the elements of mass, rhythm, design, and movement in the round — in three dimensions. Walk around it; sculpture is not to be seen from one side only. The sculptor sought a variety of rhythms, planes, projections, and divisions of spaces, in and out, and around. Never try to look for a realistic interpretation — pay no attention to incongruity of title. After all a title is a handle, a number in a catalogue. Sometimes it has a special meaning to the sculptor because it was the beginning of his idea, the stepping stone to creation, and he remembers this fondly.

The exaggerations of relationships and planes and forms — the semi-association with the human form — are juxtaposed to create power and expression. Sculpture has to be seen and felt.

A work of art should fire the imagination and stimulate one's intellectual and emotional reactions. If it does not do this, there is a deficiency in the observer or in the artist. A modest and serious person often thinks his lack of understanding causes a certain sculpture to mean nothing to him, whereas it may be a lack of expressive accomplishment on the part of the sculptor — or the sculpture just may not awaken a sympathetic response in him. On the other hand there are those whose minds are so closed to art expression that marvelous works of art evoke no response.

There are artists who, themselves, give all manner of fantastic and esoteric interpretations to their own work, interpretations which often belong to literature or some other medium. These have often served as a fly wheel or starter for their flights of fancy leading to sculptural expression, but the sculpture has to stand on its own feet unsupported by literary interpretation. Sculpture is a language in itself, its words are not the words of literature or music. Art is a profound feeling for nature and life. The thing created must live as an entity in itself. There must be love for the material and for the idea expressed through this material. A living breath goes into the stone or bronze, the quality of being removed from the temporary into the eternal.

Modern sculpture — by this I mean the sculpture of today — has had some recognition by museums, some government sponsorship in Franklin

11

D. Roosevelt's time, and some little private support. But we do not find it on our buildings or in our parks or even in our homes. Architecture has become so functional and streamlined that it ignores sculpture. Yet modern architecture and modern sculpture complement and enhance each other — both use light and shade, textures, daring and simplified design, and new and exciting materials. Architects and clients to the contrary, architecture needs sculpture and America is full of young and vigorous sculptors eager to adorn our buildings.

When a person wants to know what is being done in sculpture in these United States today, what does he do? If he is in New York and goes to the Metropolitan Museum he will find a dozen not too representative pieces. If he goes to the Modern Museum he will find a greater number — and more modern pieces. If he is lucky enough to come at the time of the Whitney Museum's sculpture show, he will get some idea of our sculpture. Or he may find a one-man show of sculpture at one of the galleries and can really familiarize himself with the artist's work. But he can go no farther. American sculpture will seem very sparse and American sculptors a feeble minority.

Yet America is full of sculptors. There are hundreds of sculptors working in this country. There is a group of older and established sculptors and an army of young, vigorous and accomplished sculptors; and, beyond them, innumerable students and potential sculptors. The young sculptors are to be found not only in New York and the big cities. They are all over the country and are alive, experimental, courageous and filled with creative spirit. Yet few know them or their work. It is not in museums or in books, nor is it in our homes. Yet nothing speaks of the culture and taste and intelligence of the people who live in a house or apartment as do the pictures on their walls and the sculpture which they display. "By their art shall you know them."

Brummé has felt so deeply this need for someone to present American sculpture to the American people that he has compiled this book. It is fresh and comprehensive and impersonal. I am sure Brummé is intensely interested in the more modern directions and expressions of contemporary art, being vigorous and alive and young; but he does not allow this to limit his awareness of the many directions of sculptural expression. He presents a rounded picture of sculpture today. Comprehensive as this book is, I am sure there were again as many sculptors whom he wanted to include yet could not because of the limitation of space.

It has been truly said that to talk of French sculpture and English sculpture and American sculpture is absurd. It is all sculpture (good, or bad or mediocre). There are still traces of national characteristics in art but in this day of intimate communication, art is universal and tribal differences so slight as to be no more than a flavor. The directions, the possibilities of form are understood by all sculptors working in this medium. But there are American sculptors, a lively, dynamic tribe of them and Brummé presents them to America in all their variety and accomplishment. This is a most important book and a badly needed book. People of these United States, meet and know your sculptors!

PREFACE AND NOTE ON SELECTION

THIS is the first comprehensive survey of contemporary American sculpture, free of stylistic and organizational limitation.

The increased activity in the Arts in the United States, which, I dare say, borders strongly on a renaissance, has projected on the scene of American culture many excellent and many promising young sculptors.

Having closely observed this art form develop over the past twenty years, seeing it grow constantly stronger, more imaginative, creative and original, seeing it absorb from and build well on the foundations of the modern movement in Europe, I felt that my enthusiasms and deep appreciation would be shared by many if a survey in book form were made. I was impelled, also, by the fact that the opportunity of viewing much sculpture is confined to those of us living in metropolitan centers.

In this survey emphasis is, of course, placed on the younger sculptors, for the task of further developing a contemporary esthetic direction is primarily theirs. Fadism and playful dadaistic toys, such as the "fur-lined tea cup" epitomized, I have purposely eliminated. Fortunately, such decadence and neuroses are found only in a very limited group. On the other hand, sound, considered experiments in the vital aspects of sculpture are so widely conducted that it is impossible to represent all the fine sculptors in a single volume.

Although this is by no means intended as a history of American sculpture, but rather a survey of the contemporary scene, I have felt it fitting to include posthumously the work of several excellent sculptors.

Whereas I had originally prepared a great deal of text, I have eliminated all but a few pages in order to present more visual material. Critical standards, therefore, are manifested in my selection of sculptures, instead of verbal commentary.

Also, with regard to the text, I have avoided abstruse intellectual theories. In preference, I have sought to feel and interpret the pulse and thought pattern of our society which, of necessity, is the crucible whence originate the art forms of our time. Their ingredients are basic intellectual and emotional experiences common to all. Furthermore, we should all be historically familiar with the art forms and the social and political mores inspiring them in other epochs. Therefore, I felt that a simple clarification of this same transposition of art and society, as applied to the contemporary scene, would be best for stimulating a deeper enjoyment and increased understanding of the rich expressions of contemporary American sculpture.

Another feature upon which I have placed great stress and to which I have devoted much of this space, is the bibliography of two hundred and fifty-odd volumes of international contemporary sculpture, esthetics, the techniques of sculpture, and monographs and surveys of earlier periods of American sculpture. This bibliography is, to my knowledge, the most comprehensive in the English language.

In conclusion, I would like to express the hope that the regrettable interference with the freedom of the Arts, throughout history, by those inadequately schooled in the Arts and Humanities may never be repeated.

C. Ludwig Brummé

New York, 1948

13

CONTEMPORARY AMERICAN SCULPTURE

To enjoy and understand to the fullest extent the period in which we live, an appreciation of contemporary art forms must play an important role. Contemporary American sculpture is being created, as was the sculpture of past eras, for the inspiration of the people.

It is difficult to reconcile with a twentieth century existence, our remaining bound to the past in matters of appreciation and participation in the Arts. The widespread practice of teaching art historically, emphasizing memory training rather than the development of an esthetic sense, has deprived many of the key to a full appreciation and understanding of contemporary American sculpture.

In our appraisal of the vitality of the sculpture of any given period, the primary factor, aside from pure esthetic considerations, is the degree of sensitivity, perception, and strength of its reflection of the philosophy and social structure of the society for which it is created. The history of man and that of sculpture run a non-deviating parallel. Man's growth and direction, decay and retrogression are indelibly written in sculpture. Preserved are the mythologies, esthetics, social and political structures of each epoch and geographically separated branch of existence, from paleolithic man to date.

One has but to look at the sculpture of Ancient Egypt or Greece, or Rome, or at the Romanesque and Gothic sculpture of the Middle Ages to see how it reflected the mores, politics, and philosophy of each period.

With the Renaissance we entered an age of individual thinking. The revival of learning and the rediscovery of ancient art caused sculptors to express themselves in a variety of themes, including ancient pagan myths and Catholic symbols. Nevertheless, with a few exceptions, this was not an important era in sculpture.

The eighteenth and nineteenth centuries introduced a new curtailment of this Renaissance-born freedom — academism. Strong men of sculpture, influenced by a revival of classical art and literature, dominated the scene. Their devotion to classicism was tantamount to any dogmatic form of religion or philosophy. Through control of schools, academies, museums, arts commissions, and art counseling, they imposed their stamp on all but a few sculptural expressions of that period. It must be granted, however, in our consideration of this period, as reflected in its sculpture, that this conformance, this lure of the glories of the past, was characteristic of its time. It was a period of kings and princes, of political and economic feudalism, of a lush, extravagant way of life, and a decorative, non-provocative art.

The latter part of the nineteenth century, however, proved more restive. Rodin, and the circle he inspired, fired the embers of artistic revolution into flame. Although their influence was internationally felt, their quest for freedom and greater breadth of sculptural expressions did not carry the strength of the corresponding period of impressionism in painting. Academism was too strong numerically. Only a few sculptors risked their reputations and patronage by seeking new departures.

Were we then to have a sculpture reflecting our time and its vitality, its imagination and search for broadened horizons, we could not find it in this continued traditionalism. Additional prophets and new directions were needed to free this art from its long cycle of stagnation. This sculptural evolution was, of course, inevitable. For art, as life, can never be static. It reflects the heterogeneous civilizations of advancing history. With the beginning of the twentieth century the sculptors, destined to lead in the development of a contemporary esthetic philosophy in sculpture, appeared. In Europe there were Archipenko, Brancusi, Boccioni, Duchamp-Villon, Epstein, Gaudier-Brzeska, and Lehmbruck; and later Arp, Barlach, de Creeft, Gabo, Gargallo, Giacometti, Laurens, Lipchitz, Moore, Pevsner, Vantongerloo, and others; while in the United States were such men as Lachaise, Laurent, and Zorach.

Assimilation and development are two qualities characteristic of our time. This is also true in the field of sculpture. Clearly apparent in the work of the contemporary European and American sculptors is a union of the vigor, sensitivity, and creativeness of the sculpture of all peoples. No longer are they confined to a sculpture concept limited to classical civilizations. On the contrary, they have found inspiration in the simplicity and freer use of form in the sculptures of the peoples of Africa and Oceania, of the pre-Columbian civilizations such as the Mayan and Aztec, of the artistic North American Indian, and of the Orient. This broadened perspective plus the findings of twentieth century experimenters in pure form have engendered the esthetic philosophy of form needed in our age of individual expression. Thus we come to the core of meaning of contemporary American sculpture.

Were there one dominant, isolated mythology governing the American thought pattern, which the American sculptor interpreted, as did the Egyptian, the Greek, the Roman, and others, contemporary sculpture would likewise be monostylistic and thematic. This, however, is not the case. Our society is a complexity of multilateral political, social, and religious beliefs and organizations.

This, then, is the key to the many-styled expressions of contemporary American sculpture. Of the same cloth as our own belief in freedom, is the weave of the sculptors' varied esthetic patterns. They do not serve any one political or religious group. They express themselves, their social and artistic consciousness, according to their own artistic philosophy, be it classical or modern. Neither are they bound by any social preference, artistic dogma, or precedent. They refuse to cater to tastes which in matters of art are bound by the past five centuries. Theirs is the strength of conviction and patience needed to convert the public to a sculptural re-evaluation, to a truly reflective and perceptive consciousness in sculpture, such as has always distinguished a period of growth and vitality from periods of passive repetition or outright decadence.

These are merely some of the influences on American sculpture today: the advances of science, the changes in our social structure and social behavior, the wider understanding of the human body and mind resulting from the development of psychology and psychoanalysis, industrialization and ever-widening use and knowledge of machines.

In addition, contemporary sculpture is increasingly successful in symbolizing the spiritual forces beyond the obvious surface. Nor does it strive to please by catering to instant recognition and memory. On the contrary, it strives, through the impact of its forms and rhythms and vitality, to provoke thought processes and emotions more deeply rooted in the human psyche than surface memory.

Each sculptor attempts, through his own expression, and whatever style he wishes or chooses to originate, to interpret our time and its moments of beauty, its periods of struggle and tragedy. Richly represented are expressions in all the so-called styles: classicism, romanticism, neoclassicism, expressionism, social realism, abstractionism, surrealism, nonobjectivism, and whatever variations of these styles may be known by other names.

These works portray well the definition of types of sculpture used by R. H. Wilenski in *The Meaning of Modern Sculpture*:

"a. Sculpture with a magic purpose, sculpture with a religious purpose, sculpture with a propaganda purpose, sculpture with a narrative purpose; b. sculpture which owes part of its appearance to the will of persons other than the sculptor; c. sculpture which owes its appearance entirely to the sculptor's will.

"*It admits though it does not demand* the representation of physical objects (human beings, animals, trees, etc.) and concrete things."

Here, I should also like to point to the wealth and range of the materials employed by these sculptors. This is a physical aspect of our sculpture giving it a color and character never before achieved. Pertinent also is the fact that all the sculptures in stone and wood are, with but two or three exceptions, direct carvings.

There is in the work of all these sculptors an integrity and an appeal to beauty and truth, which permit their eloquent flow and which teach us to appreciate the things that are honest, human, and beautiful. They also voice a warning to a world where beauty and philosophy no longer seem important, or are subjected to oppression; for such a world, as seen in recent history, can bring only tragedy and suffering to its people.

I can but reaffirm that contemporary American sculpture does, without question, reflect our time, our search for greater freedom and more lasting values, for a twentieth century morality and equality, for an internationalism of brotherhood and peace, just as clearly as Greek sculpture reflected the literary greatness and paganism of the Greeks; Roman sculpture, the lust for power and chauvinism of the Romans; and the Gothic period, the era of Christendom.

Plates

GEORGE AARONS   *Bronze*

JEREMIAH

Plate 1

HUMBERT ALBRIZIO   *Cherry Wood*

SEATED FIGURE

Courtesy Kraushaar Galleries, New York   *Plate 2*

LEO AMINO   *Hydrostone*

RITE OF SPRING

Plate 3

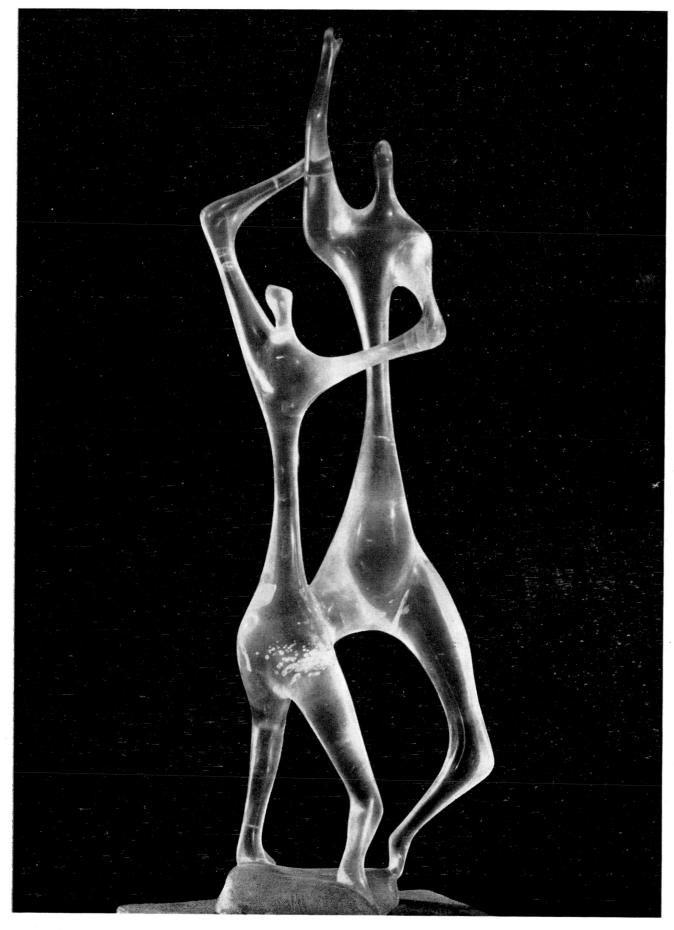

LEO AMINO   *Translucent Plastic*

SPRING

Courtesy Sculptors Gallery,
Clay Club Sculpture Center, New York   *Plate 4*

ALEXANDER ARCHIPENKO

Chromium Plated Bronze

SILHOUETTE

Plate 5

ALEXANDER ARCHIPENKO

Carved Lucite

SPACE AND LIGHT

Plate 6

SAUL BAIZERMAN   *Hammered Copper*

EXUBERANCE

Plate 7

OLIVER O'CONNOR BARRETT   *Nopowood*

REQUIEM

Collection Owen Dodson, Washington, D. C.   *Plate* 8

C. Ludwig Brummé   *Purple Heart Wood*

SOLILOQUY

Plate 9

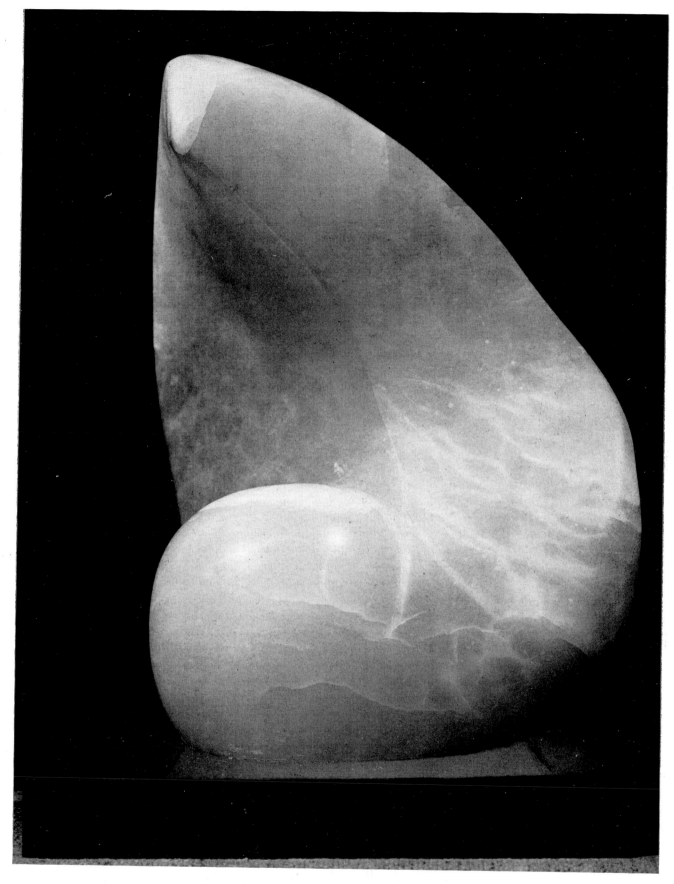

C. Ludwig Brummé

Italian Alabaster

MADONNA

Plate 10

BENIAMINO BUFANO   *Red Porphyry*

THE PRAYER

Plate 11

BENIAMINO BUFANO   *Red Porphyry*

BEARS

Plate 12

DORIS CAESAR

Bronze

WOMAN, CHILD AND HAND #1

Owned by Dr. Henry L. Blank, New York

Plate 13

DORIS CAESAR

Bronze

HUNGER

Courtesy Weyhe Gallery, New York

Plate 14

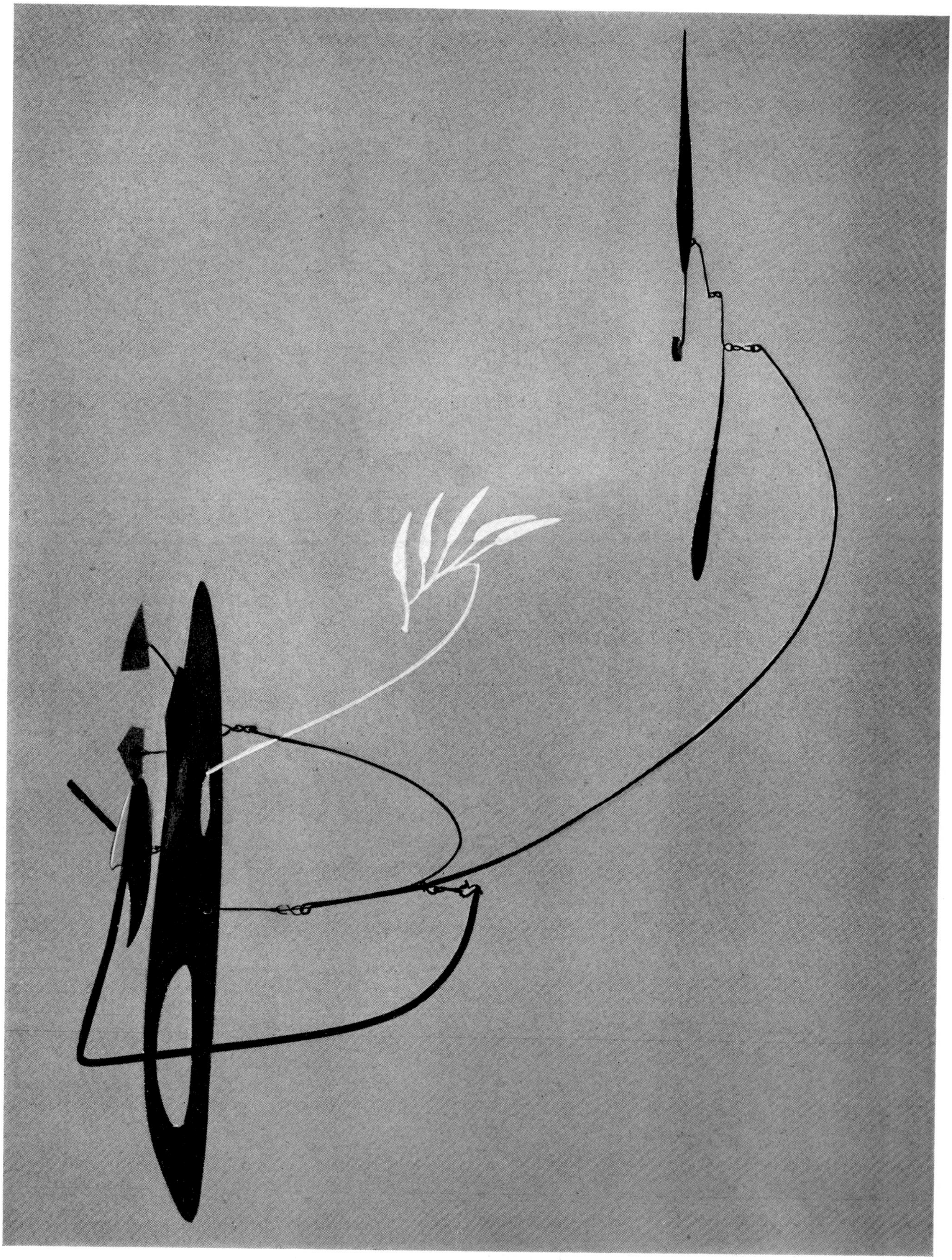

ALEXANDER CALDER

THE WHITE LILY

Steel

Collection of the City Art Museum,
St. Louis, Missouri

Plate 15

ALEXANDER CALDER

Steel

THE FOREST IS THE BEST PLACE

Plate 16

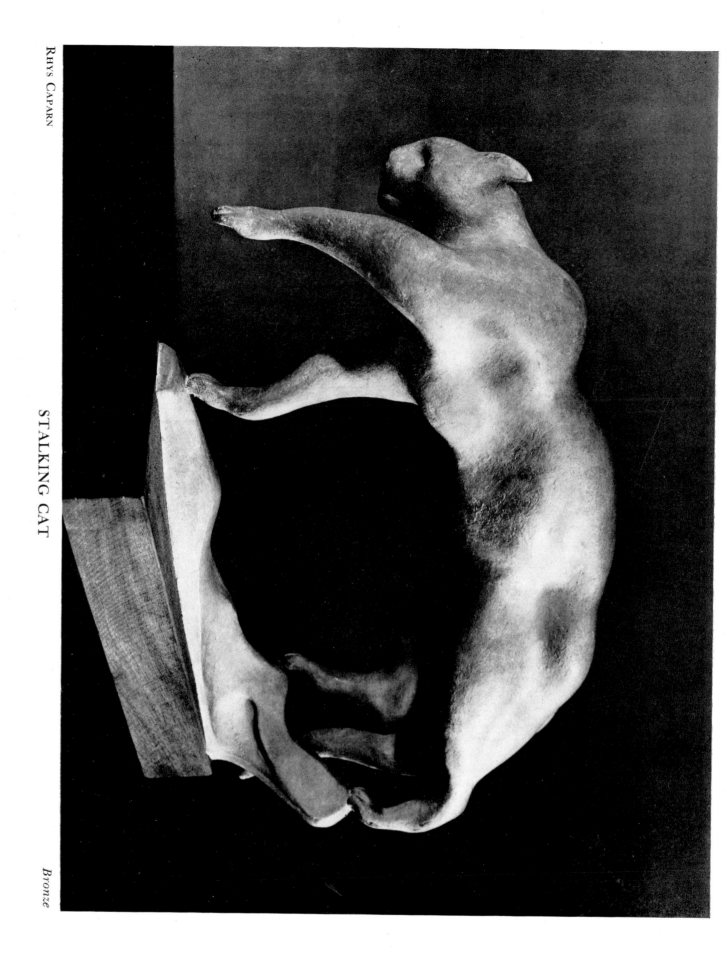

RHYS CAPARN

STALKING CAT

Bronze

Courtesy Wildenstein & Co., Inc., New York

Plate 17

ALBINO CAVALLITO

Black Belgian Marble

SEAL

Courtesy Sculptors Gallery,
Clay Club Sculpture Center, New York

Plate 18

GEORGE CERNY

Red Sienna Marble

REVERIE

Courtesy Sculptors Gallery,
Clay Club Sculpture Center, New York

Plate 19

Black Belgian Marble

VIXEN

George Cerny

Plate 20

GLENN CHAMBERLAIN

WOUNDED BIRD

Driftwood

Courtesy Sculptors Gallery,
Clay Club Sculpture Center, New York

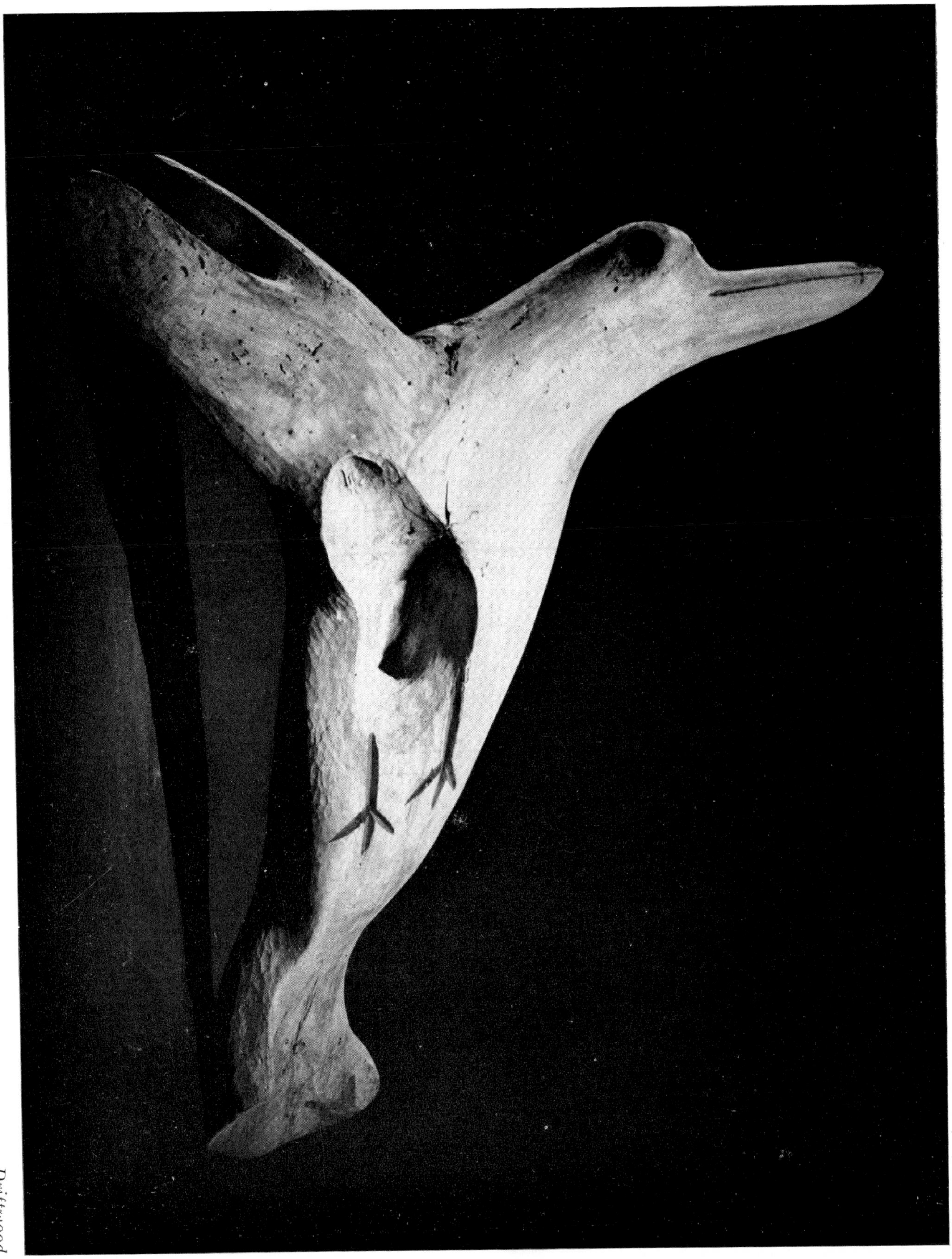

Plate 21

Granite

MERMAID

Collection of the Virginia Museum of Fine Arts,
Richmond, Virginia

Plate 22

Jo Davidson   *Original Clay*

ALBERT EINSTEIN

Plate 23

Jo Davidson   *Original Clay*

FRANKLIN DELANO ROOSEVELT

Plate 24

José de Creeft   Hammered Lead

RACHMANINOFF

Courtesy Georgette Passedoit Gallery, New York   *Plate 25*

José de CREEFT

Black Belgian Granite

MAYA

Plate 26

Marina Nunez Del Prado   *Walnut*

LLAMAS

Courtesy Associated American Artists, Inc., New York   *Plate 27*

DONALD DE LUE   *Plaster for Bronze*

EVE

Plate 28

JEAN DE MARCO   *Tennessee Marble*

INDIAN WOMAN

Plate 29

JEAN DE MARCO   *Copper Repoussé, 9′*

CHRIST AND HIS APOSTLES

Courtesy Sculptors Gallery,
Clay Club Sculpture Center, New York   *Plate 30*

José de RIVERA

YELLOW — BLACK

Painted Aluminum

Courtesy Mortimer Levitt Gallery, New York

Plate 31

José de Rivera BLACK – RED – YELLOW *Painted Aluminum*

Courtesy Mortimer Levitt Gallery, New York

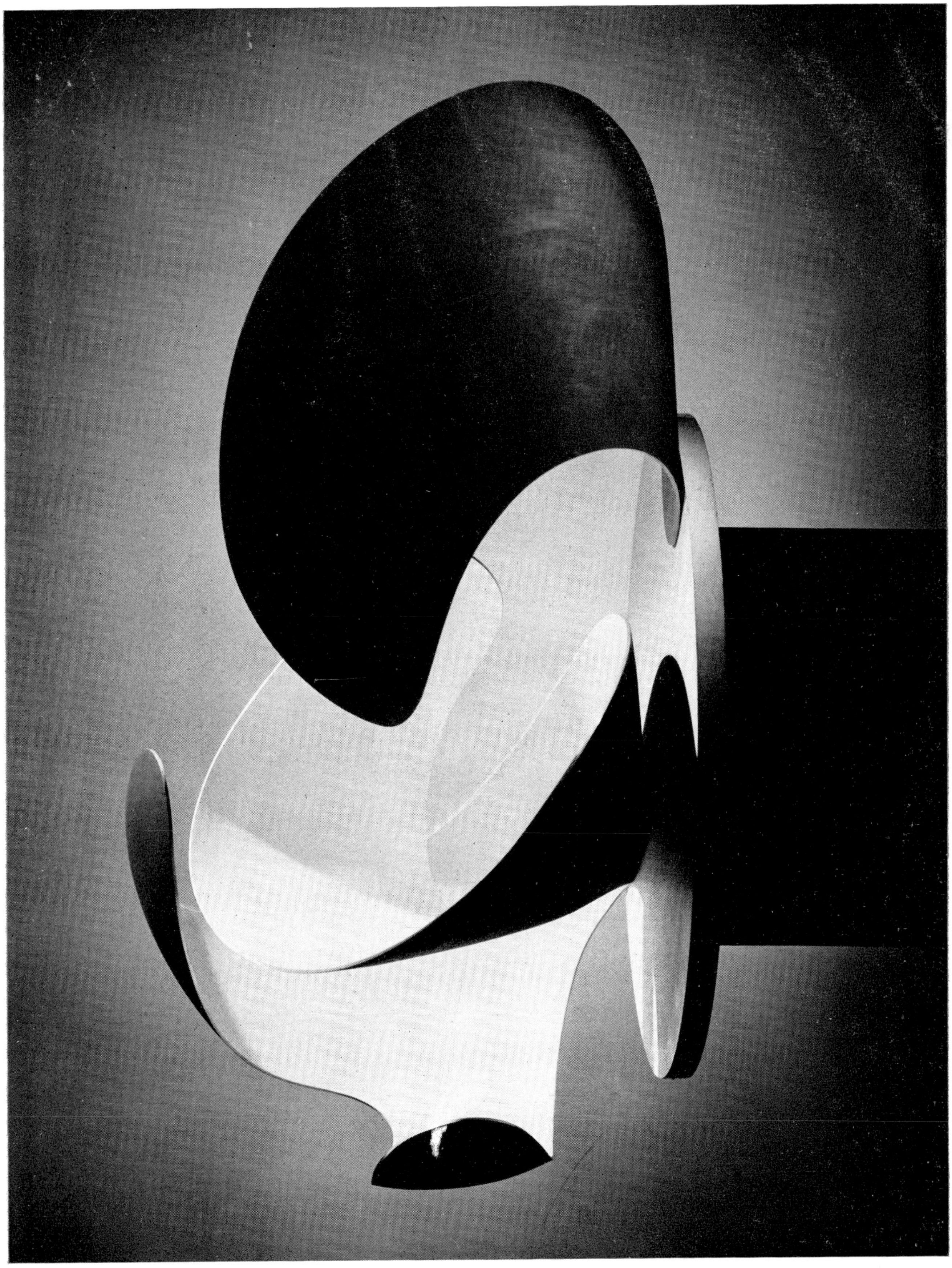

LEDA AND THE SWAN

White Alabama Marble

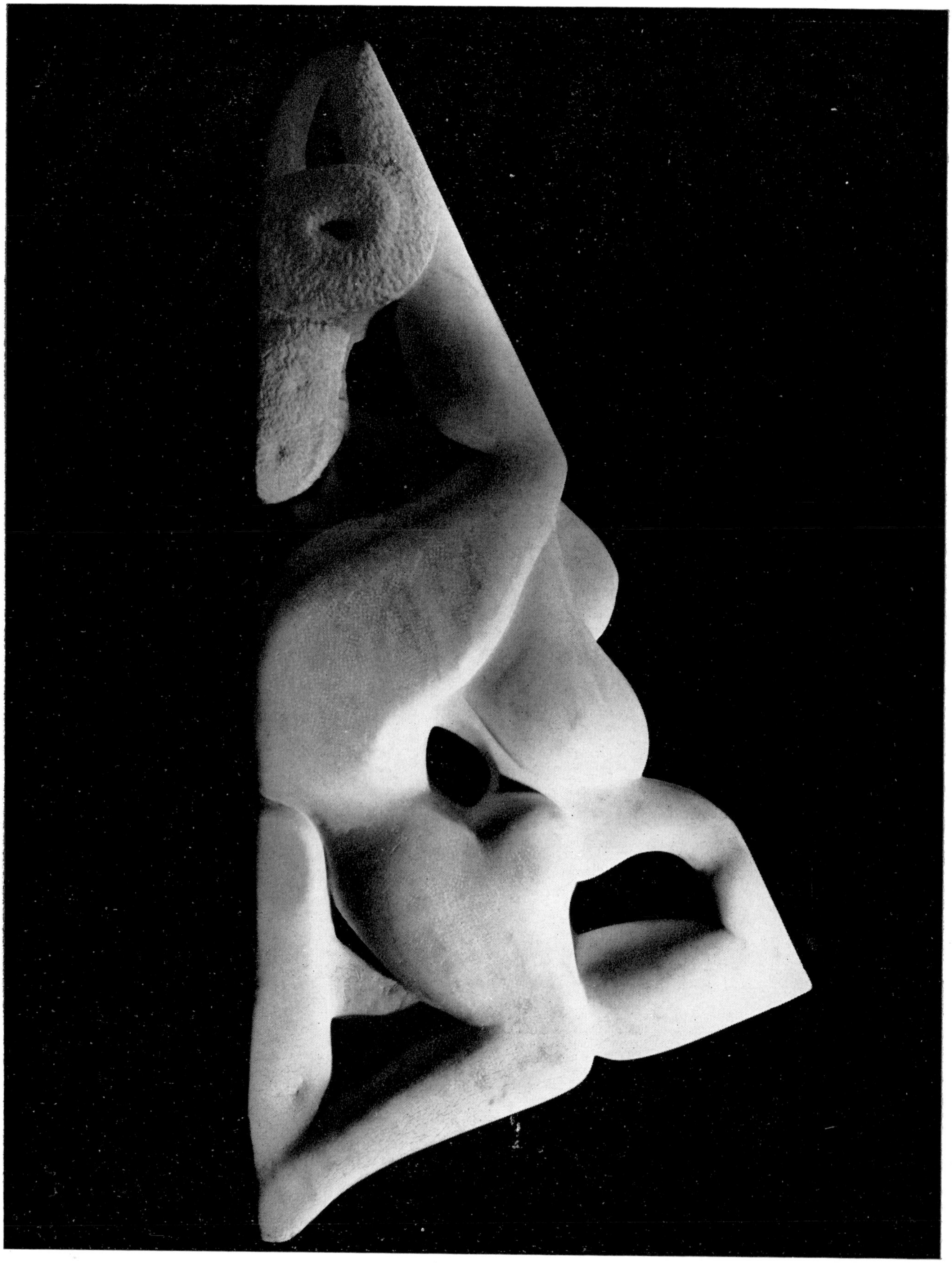

Plate 33

KOREN DER HAROOTIAN   *Westfield Green Marble*

PROMETHEUS AND THE VULTURE

         Plate 34

BLANCHE DOMBEK

Snakewood

UNITY

Courtesy Sculptors Gallery,
Clay Club Sculpture Center, New York

Plate 35

BLANCHE DOMBEK

Brazilian Rosewood

THE DETERMINANT

Courtesy Sculptors Gallery,
Clay Club Sculpture Center, New York

Plate 36

Lu Duble

Plaster for Bronze

EL PENITENTE

Plate 37

LU DUBLE

Plaster for Bronze

FUNERAL DANCER

Plate 38

JACOB EPSTEIN

Bronze

GEORGE BERNARD SHAW

Courtesy Maynard Walker Gallery, New York

Plate 39

MOTHER AND CHILD

 Plate 40

ALFEO FAGGI   *Terra Cotta*

XIII STATION OF THE CROSS

In the Church of St. Thomas The Apostle, Chicago, Ill.   *Plate 41*

CLARA FASANO   *Cement*

WOMAN AND CHILD

Plate 42

AGGRESSIVE ACT

Lead

Plate 43

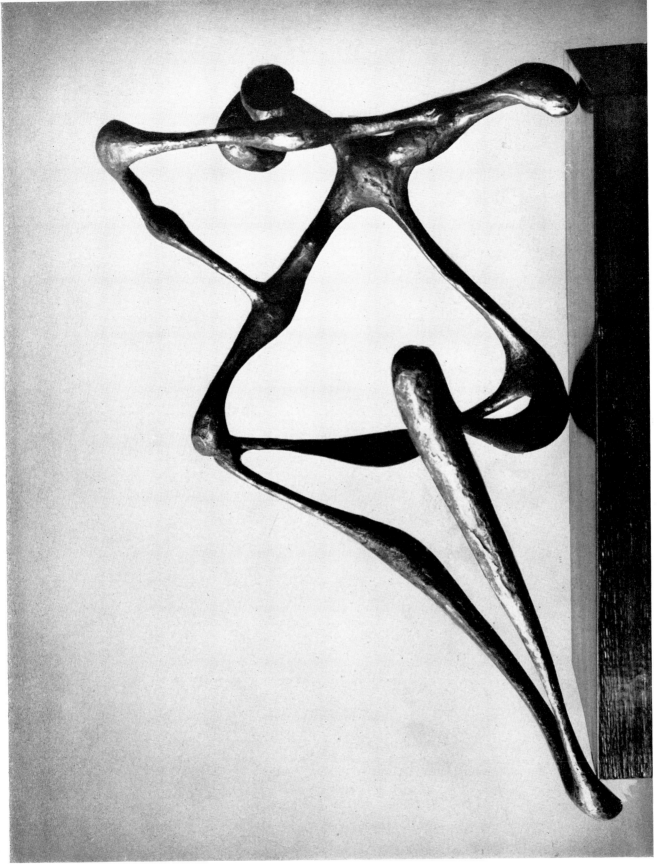

METAMORPHOSIS

HERBERT FERBER

Plate 44

JOHN B. FLANNAGAN   *Fieldstone with Brass Tail*

BRASS TAIL MONKEY #1

Owned by Mr. and Mrs. Wladimir Selinsky, New York   *Plate 45*

JOHN B. FLANNAGAN   *Granite*

DUCK

VINCENT GLINSKY

THE AWAKENING

Carrara Marble

Plate 47

THE AWAKENING (REAR VIEW)

VINCENT GLINSKY

Plate 48

AARON J. GOODELMAN   *Tennessee Pink Marble*

HAPPY LANDING

Plate 49

AARON J. GOODELMAN   *Wild Cherry Wood*

MY KIN

Courtesy A. C. A. Gallery, New York   *Plate 50*

DOROTHEA GREENBAUM

THE SNOB

Limestone

Plate 51

Bronze

SYMBOLIC FIGURE # IV

PETER GRIPPE

Courtesy Willard Gallery, New York

Plate 52

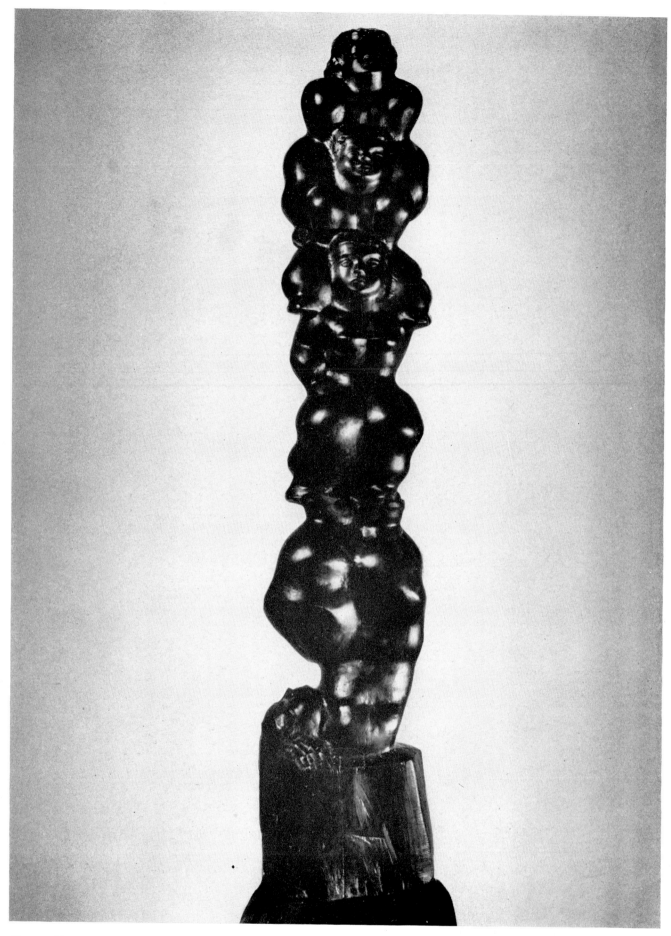

CHAIM GROSS

Ebony

FAMILY OF FOUR

Courtesy Associated American Artists, Inc., New York

Plate 53

CHAIM GROSS

Lithium Stone

ETERNAL MOTHER

Plate 54

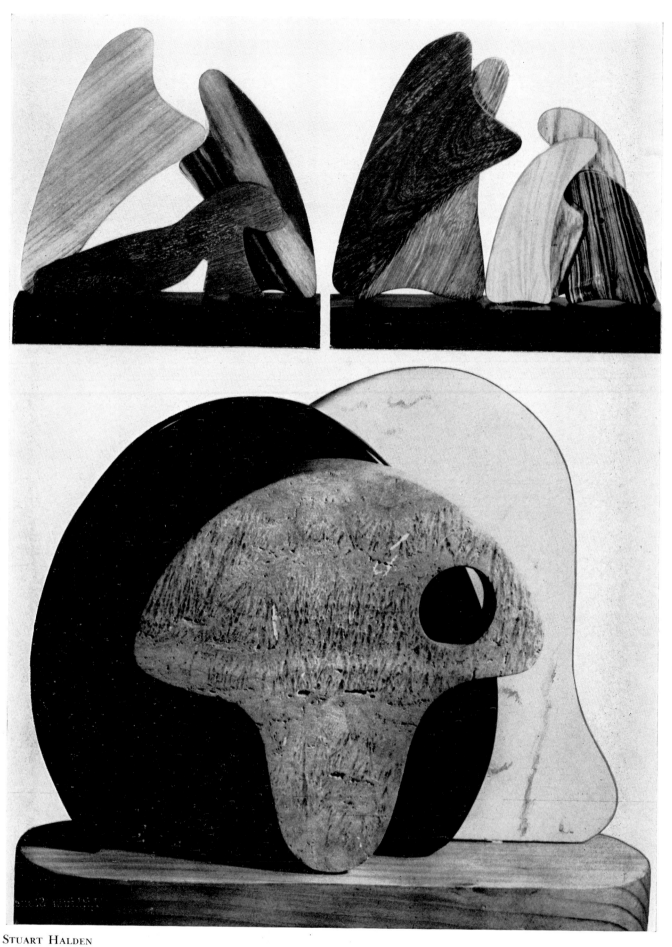

STUART HALDEN

VII STATION OF THE CROSS   *Amaranth, Walnut, Heart of Ebony, Ebony*
VIII STATION OF THE CROSS *Amaranth, Guiana Rosewood, Tulip, Apple, Violet Wood and Ebony*
ARIES   *Vermont White, Belgian Black, Brown Travertine Marbles*
Courtesy Sculptors Gallery, Clay Club Sculpture Center, New York   *Plates 55, 56*

DAVID HARE

Cast Stone

HUNGRY

FRIGHTENED BIRD

Wax

Plate 58

MINNA HARKAVY   *Bronze*

WOMAN IN THOUGHT

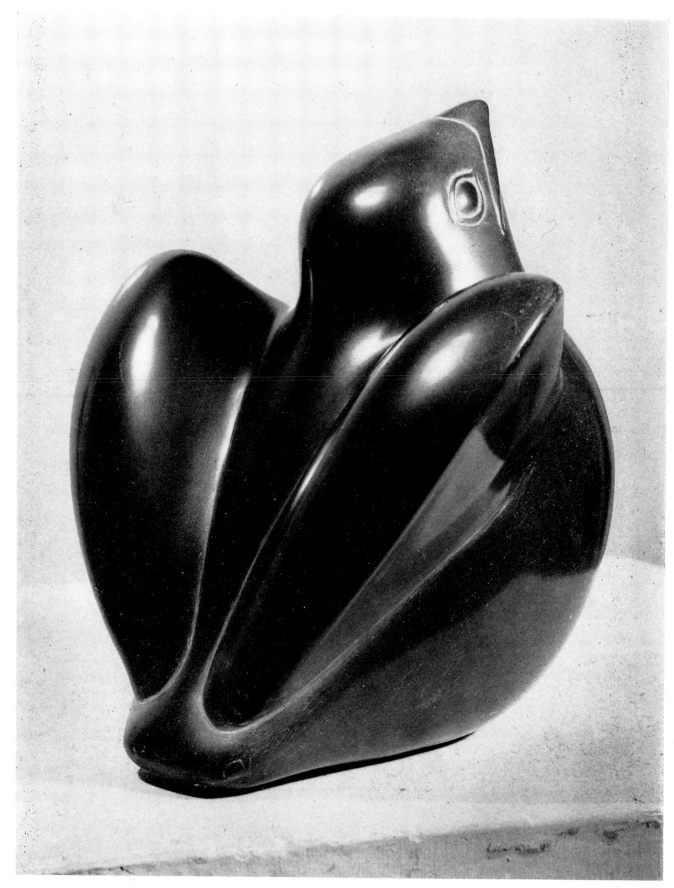

CLEO HARTWIG   *Black Belgian Marble*

FLEDGLING

Collection of Mrs. William W. Crocker,
Burlingame, California

Plate 60

Hesketh   *Italian Olivewood*   Milton Hebald   *Tulip Wood*

SALOMÉ   MORE RICH IN HOPE

Courtesy Ferargil Galleries, New York Plate 62   Plate 61

MALVINA HOFFMAN

Limestone

WENDELL L. WILLKIE

*Collection of the Corcoran Gallery of Art,
Washington, D.C.*

Plate 63

MALVINA HOFFMAN   *Black Belgian Marble*

MARTINIQUE GIRL

Plate 64

DONAL HORD

Black Diorite

EL COLORADO

Plate 65

DONAL HORD   *Black Diorite*

AZTEC

Owned by San Diego State College,
San Diego, California   *Plate 66*

JOHN HOVANNES   *Plaster for Bronze*

RACING CYCLISTS

Plate 67

JOHN HOVANNES   *Plaster for Bronze*

STEVEDORES

Plate 68

RANDOLPH W. JOHNSTON

Bronze

FIVE THAT ESCAPED

Courtesy Sculptors Gallery,
Clay Club Sculpture Center, New York

Plate 69

MAX KALISH

Bronze

LABORER AT REST

Plate 70

Margaret Brassler Kane

Limewood

SYMBOLS OF CHANGING MAN

Plate 71

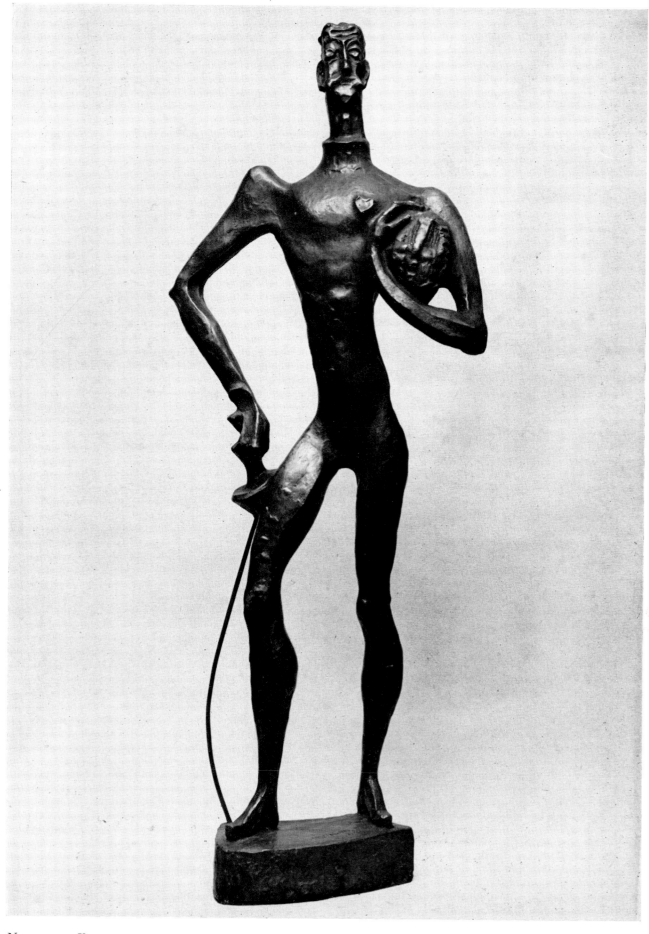

NATHANIEL KAZ   *Bronze*

DON QUIXOTE

Courtesy Associated American Artists Inc., New York   *Plate* 72

RECLINING HALF-NUDE

Limestone

Courtesy Sculptors Gallery,
Clay Club Sculpture Center, New York

Plate 73

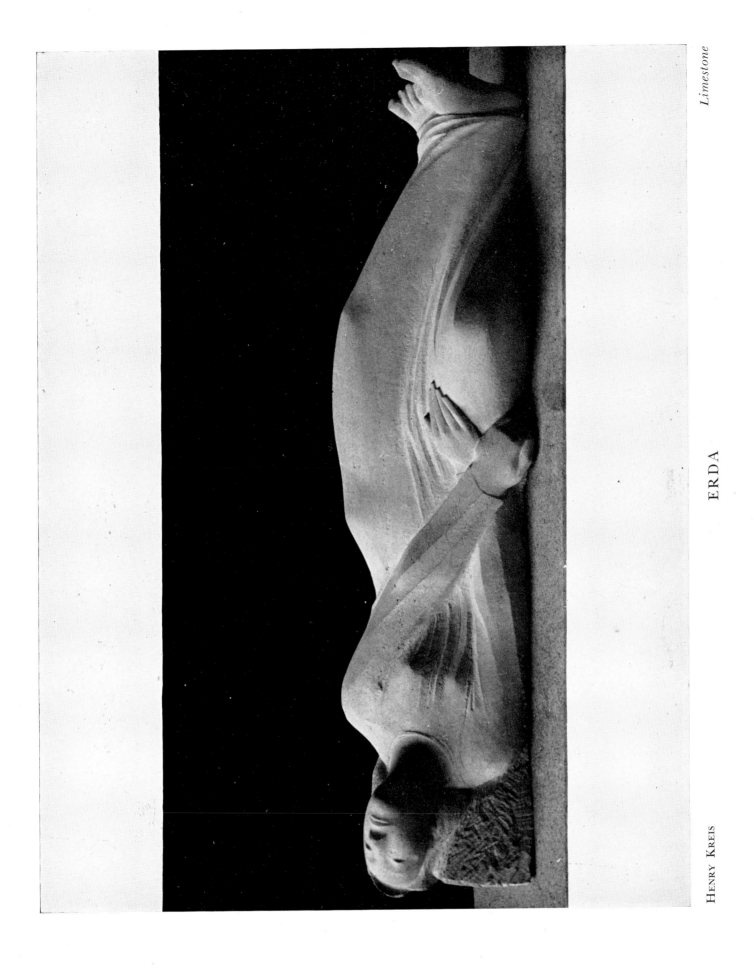

Limestone

ERDA

Henry Kreis

Plate 74

FLYING FIGURES

Bronze

Plate 75

Bronze

PORTRAIT OF JOHN MARIN

Plate 76

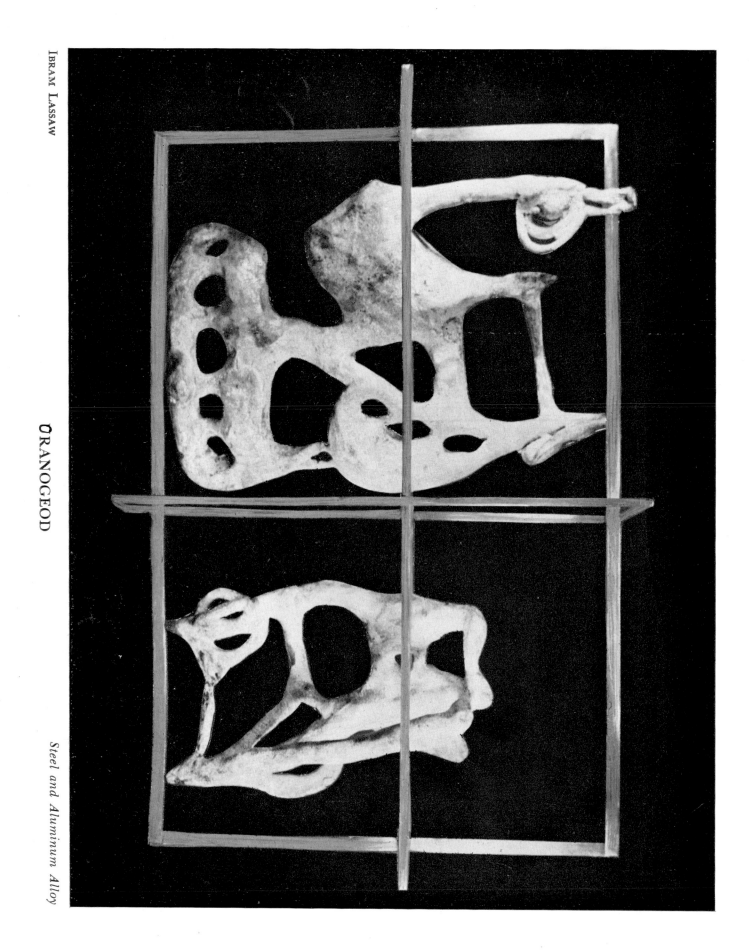

IBRAM LASSAW

ORANOGEOD

Steel and Aluminum Alloy

Courtesy Sculptors Gallery,
Clay Club Sculpture Center, New York

Plate 77

IBRAM LASSAW

Steel and Lucite

INTERSECTING RECTANGLES

Courtesy Sculptors Gallery,
Clay Club Sculpture Center, New York

Plate 78

EUROPA

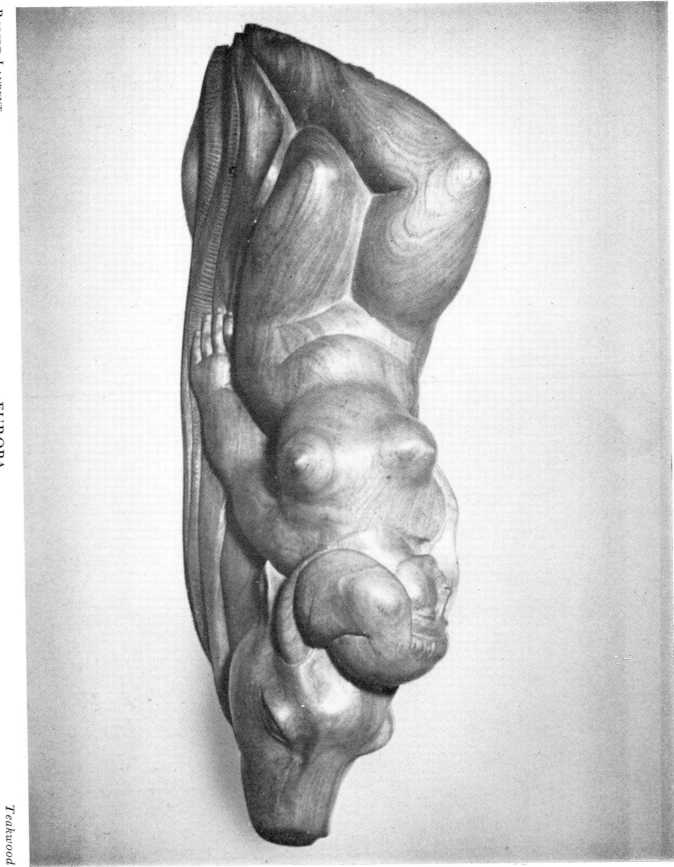

Teakwood

Plate 79

ROBERT LAURENT   *Italian Alabaster*

LA TOILETTE

Plate 80

WHISPER

Brass and Copper Wire

Plate 81

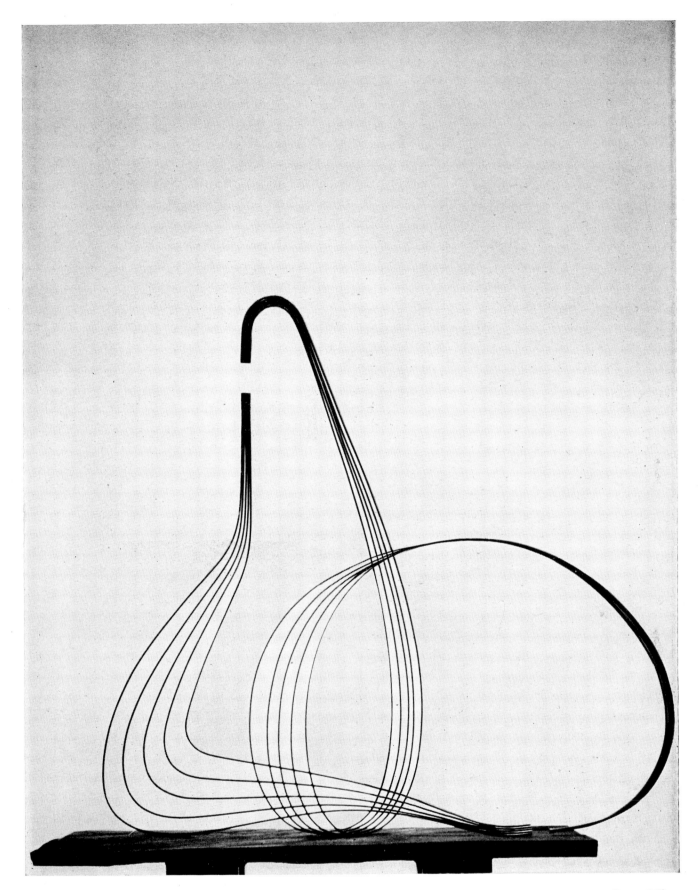

RICHARD LIPPOLD   *Brass Wire*

EMBRACE

Courtesy Willard Gallery, New York   *Plate* 82

SEYMOUR LIPTON   *Lead Construction*

MOLOCH # II

SEYMOUR LIPTON   *Lead Construction*

INVOCATION

Courtesy Betty Parsons Gallery, New York   *Plate 84*

JOSEPH LONZAR   *Bronze*

ARIEL

Plate 85

Terra Cotta

RHYTHM

Plate 86

Oronzio Maldarelli

Limestone

THE PROFESSOR

Plate 87

Oronzio Maldarelli   Carrara Marble

BIANCA

PAUL MANSHIP   *Bronze*

DIANA

Collection Brookgreen Gardens, Georgetown, South Carolina   *Plate 89*

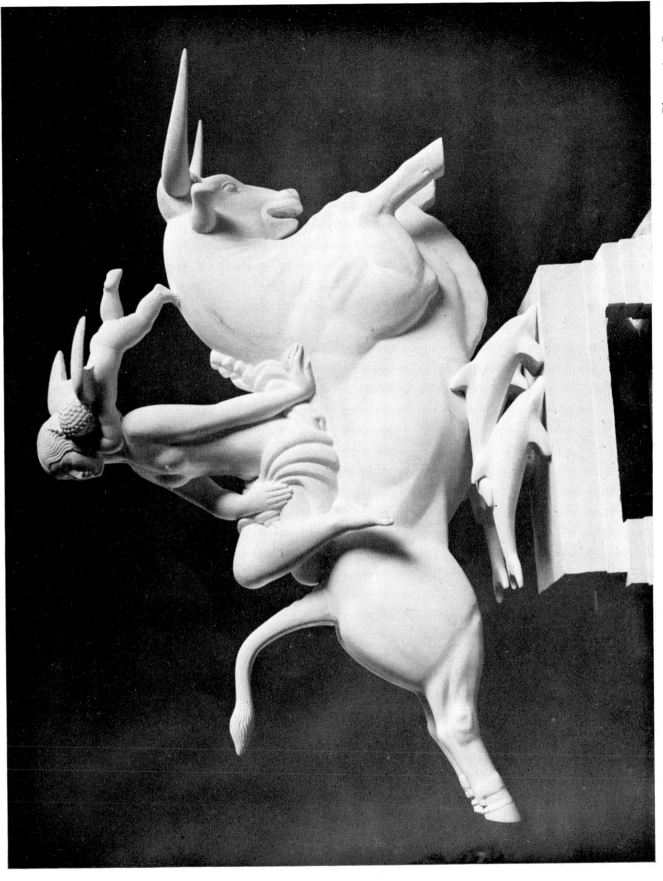

EUROPA

PAUL MANSHIP

Plate 90

MINE DISASTER

Bronze

Plate 91

Octavio Medellin   *Cast Stone*

THE PENITENTS

Plate 92

WOUNDED BULL

Bronze

STANDING BULL

ELIE NADELMAN

Plate 94

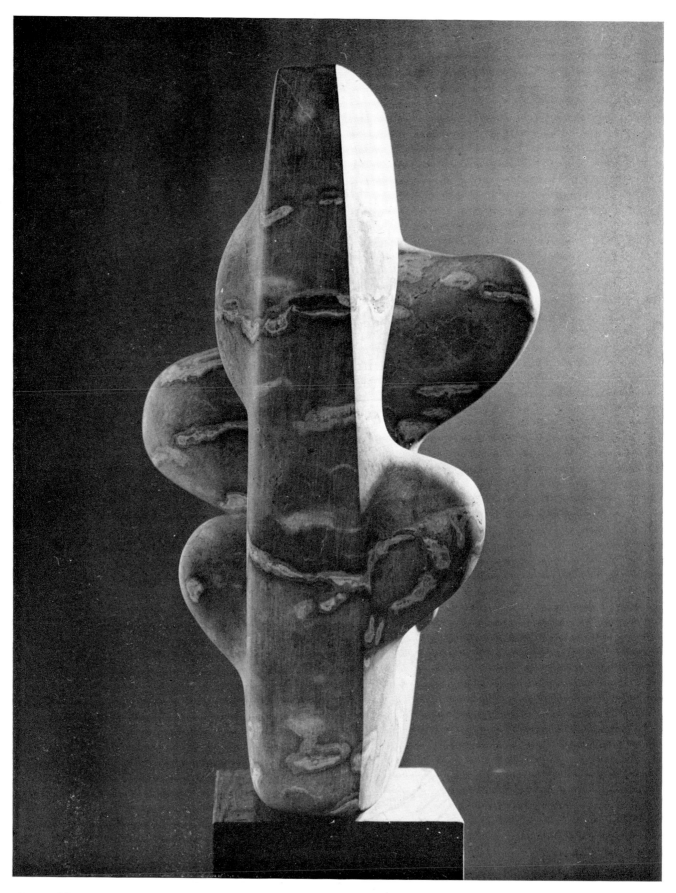

ISAMU NOGUCHI

Rouge de Vitrolis

TIME LOCK

Plate 95

ISAMU NOGUCHI   *Georgia Pink Marble*

KOUROS

Plate 96

PORCUPINE

Pale Green Quartzite

RAYMOND PUCCINELLI

BUFFALO

Diorite

Plate 98

HUGO ROBUS   *Plaster for Bronze*

SUPPLICATION

Courtesy Grand Central Art Galleries, Inc., New York   *Plate 99*

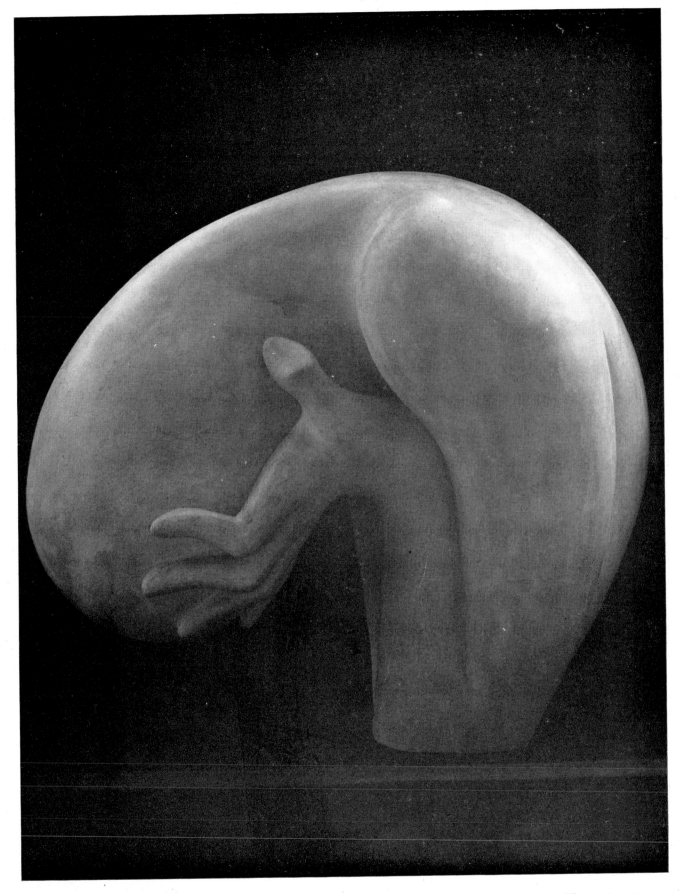

HUGO ROBUS

Plaster for Bronze

DESPAIR

Plate 100

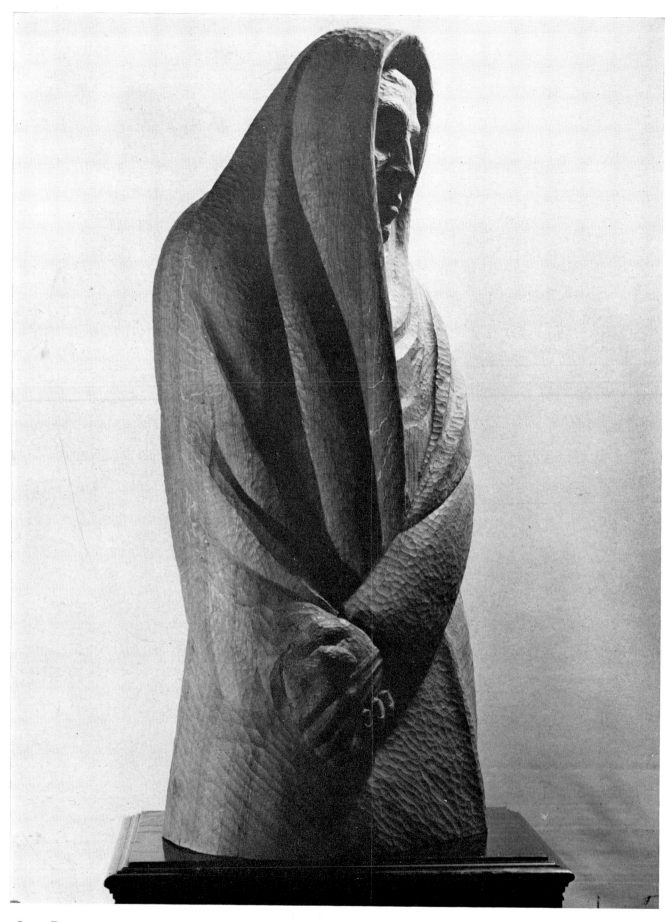

JOHN ROOD   *Oak*

WOMAN PRAYING

Courtesy Associated American Artists, Inc., New York   *Plate 101*

JOHN ROOD   *Laminated Cherry*

BOOGIE-WOOGIE BOYS

Plate 102

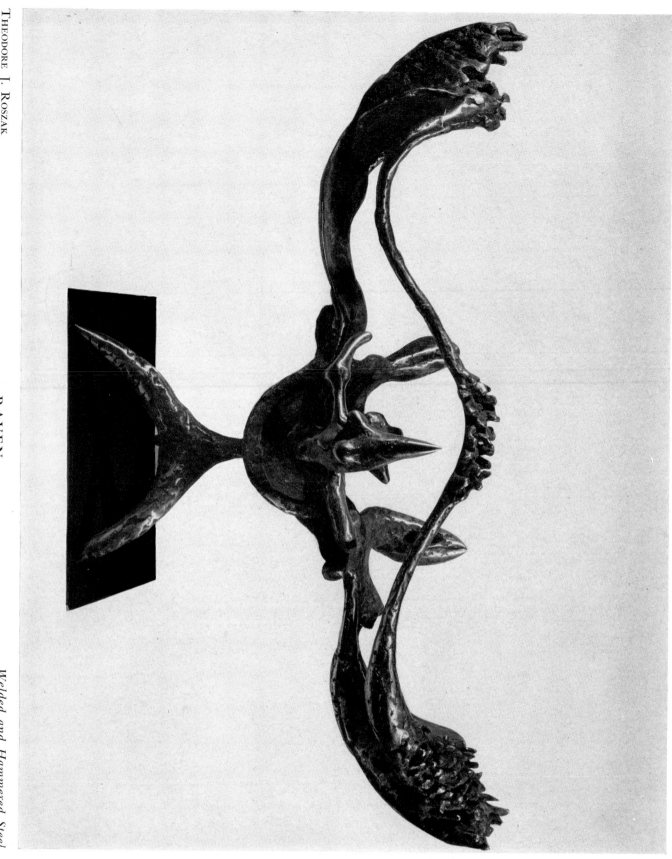

THEODORE J. ROSZAK

RAVEN

Welded and Hammered Steel

Plate 103

THEODORE J. ROSZAK

Welded and Hammered Steel

SPECTRE OF KITTY HAWK

Plate 104

HENRY ROX

Terra Cotta

YOUNG MONK

Courtesy Kleemann Galleries, New York

Plate 105

FRANCOIS H. RUBITSCHUNG   *Tennessee Pink Marble*

ONE WHO SUFFERED

Plate 106

CHARLES SALERNO

Italian Marble

SAD VICTORY

Courtesy Weyhe Gallery, New York

Plate 107

CARL L. SCHMITZ

Terra Cotta

ST. FRANCIS

Plate 108

WAR SPECTRE

Welded Steel

David Smith

Welded Steel

COCK FIGHT

Plate 110

MITZI SOLOMON   *Travertine*

GRIEF-SHAPE

Plate 111

SAHL SWARZ   *Bronze*

SEATED DANCER

Courtesy Sculptors Gallery,
Clay Club Sculpture Center, New York   *Plate* 112

CHARLES UMLAUF

PIETA

Polychromed Terra Cotta

Courtesy Mortimer Levitt Gallery, New York

Plate 113

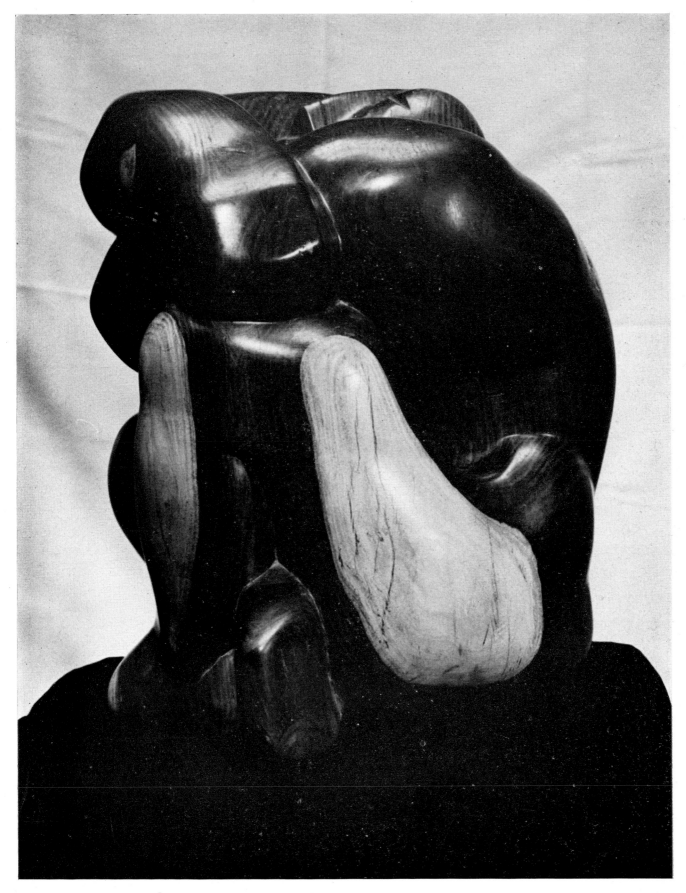

CHARLES UMLAUF   *Lignum Vitae*

MAN

POLYGNOTOS VAGIS

Carrara Marble

NIGHT

Plate 115

MARION WALTON   *Black Belgian Marble*

HEAD

Plate 116

ORANG-OUTANG THINKING

Black Belgian Marble

Collection of the Addison Gallery of American Art,
Phillips Academy, Andover, Mass.

Plate 117

HEINZE WARNECKE

Applewood

DAPHNE, ALLEGRA E PENSERIOSA

Plate 118

JANE WASEY   *Tulipwood*

THE OBSESSED

Plate 119

Black Granite

LION

SIDNEY WAUGH

Collection Brookgreen Gardens,
Georgetown, South Carolina

Plate 120

NAT WERNER
Spanish Cedar

TALMUDIST

Courtesy A. C. A. Gallery, New York
Plate 121

NAT WERNER   *Sabicu Wood*

ORGANIZER

Courtesy A. C. A. Gallery, New York   *Plate* 122

ANITA WESCHLER

A TIME TO DIE

Cast Stone

Plate 123

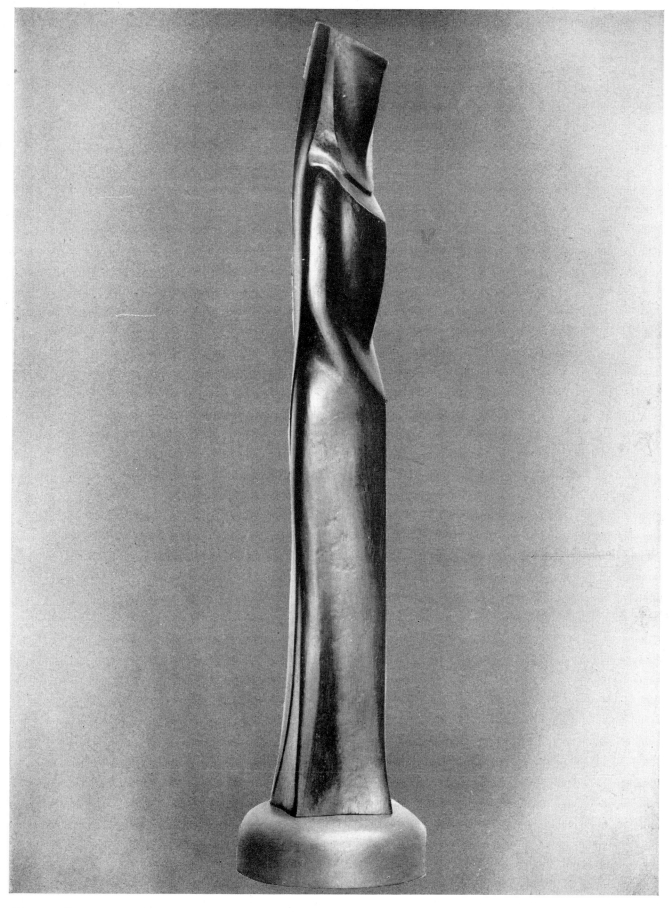

WARREN WHEELOCK   *Ebony*

THE WIDOW

Plate 124

GERTRUDE VANDERBILT WHITNEY
                                                                                    Bronze

WHEREFORE?

Plate 125

NINA WINKEL

Plaster for Bronze

ARC DE TRIOMPHE

Courtesy Sculptors Gallery
Clay Club Sculpture Center, New York

Plate 126

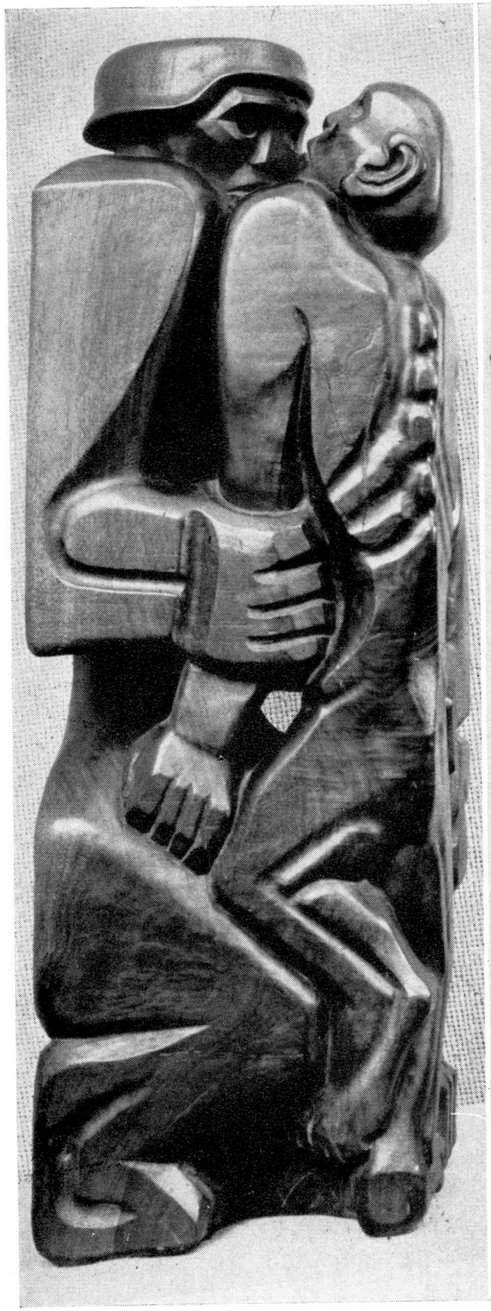

VLADIMIR YOFFE   Walnut   MAHONRI YOUNG   Bronze

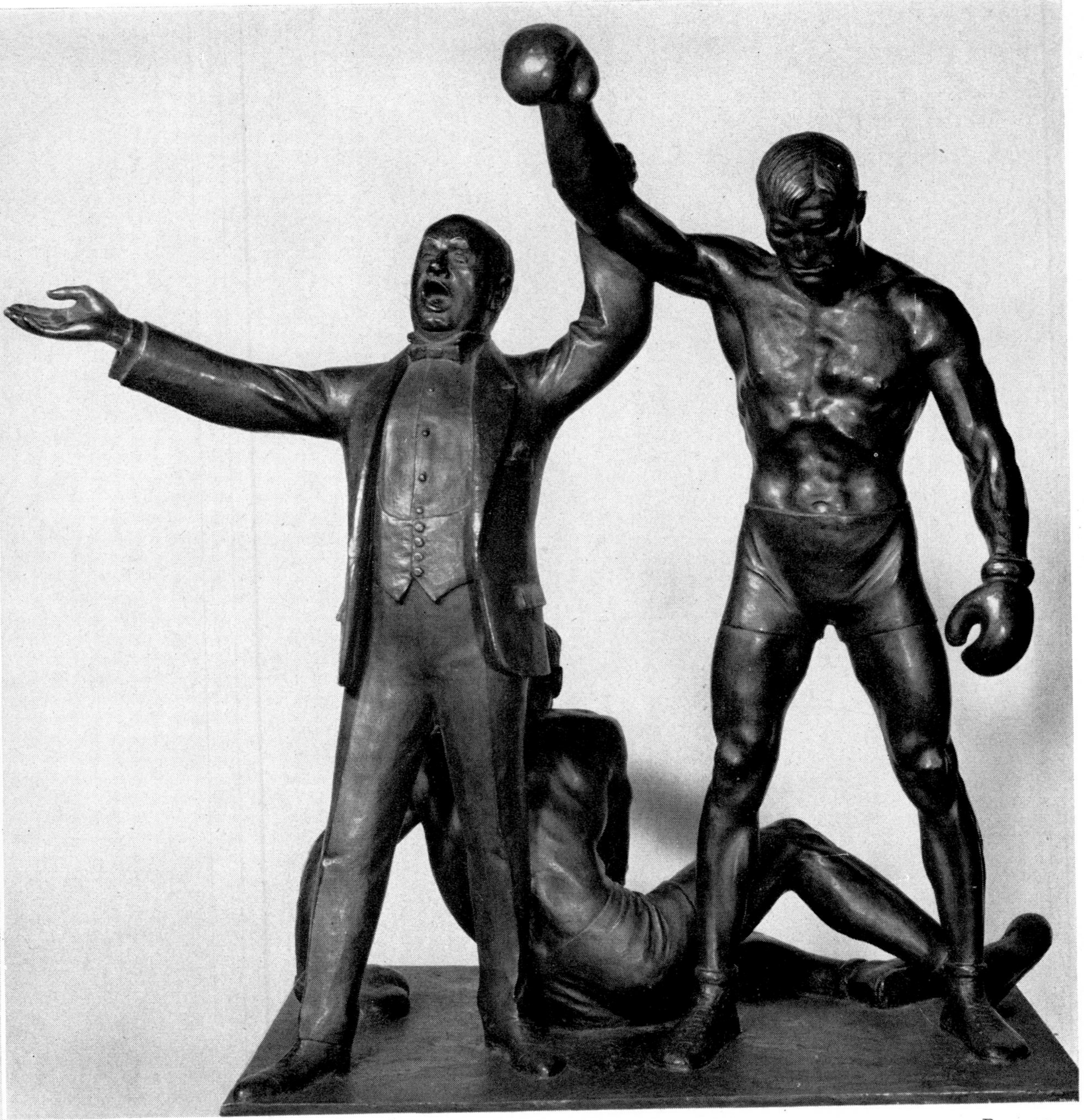

CREED OF FORCE   "DA WINNAH"

Plate 127

Plate 128

WILLIAM ZORACH   *Granite*

DEVOTION

Plate 129

WILLIAM ZORACH   *Black Granite Glacial Boulder*

THE VIRGIN

Bought by The Fine Arts Society of San Diego, California
from the Helen M. Towle Fund for the Fine Arts Gallery of San Diego   *Plate 130*

BIOGRAPHICAL NOTES

146

147

NOTE: Further biographical material, such as addresses, awards, prizes, honors, and teaching affiliations, may be found in *Who's Who in American Art*.

CONTEMPORARY AMERICAN AND EUROPEAN MONOGRAPHS AND AUTOBIOGRAPHIES

Archipenko, Alexander
Appolinaire, Guillaume. *Der Sturm*. Berlin, 1921.
........Hildebrandt, Dr. Hans. Berlin, 1923.
........Schacht, Roland. *Der Sturm*. Berlin.
........Weise, Erich. Leipzig, 1933.

Barlach, Ernst
Barlach, Ernst. *Ein Selbsterzähltes Leben*. Berlin, 1928.
........Carls, Carl Dietrich. Berlin

Barye, Antoine Louis
Metropolitan Museum of Art. New York, 1940.

Boccioni, Umberto
Coquiot, Gustave. *Cubistes, Futuristes, Passéistes*. Paris, 1914.

Bourdelle, Antoine
Catalog of Exhibition. Grand Central Art Galleries. New York, 1925.
........*Editions Nouvelle Revue Française*. Paris, 1924.

Brancusi, Constantin
Catalog of Exhibition. Brummer Gallery. Introduction, Paul Morand. New York, 1926.
........Hare, Susan. (In preparation)

Bufano, Beniamino
Catalog of Exhibition. Introduction, Roger Fry and Sam Fusco. San Francisco, 1941.

Calder, Alexander
Sweeney, James Johnson. The Museum of Modern Art. New York, 1943.

Calder, A. Stirling
Illustrated Pamphlet. Brookgreen Gardens, Georgetown, South Carolina.

Cecere, Gaetano
Illustrated Pamphlet. Brookgreen Gardens, Georgetown, South Carolina.

Daumier, Honoré
Barr, Alfred H., Jr. *Corot and Daumier*. The Museum of Modern Art. New York, 1930.

De Creeft, José
Campos, Jules. Erich S. Hermann. New York, 1945.

Degas, Edgar
Musée De L'Orangerie. Paris, 1931.

Despiau, Charles
Basler, Adolphe. Paris.
........Deshairs, Léon. Paris, 1930.
........Portfolio. The Arts Publishing Corporation. Cleveland, Ohio.

Duchamp-Villon
Librairie De France. Paris.
........Salmon, André. *Sculptures de Duchamp-Villon*. Catalog Galérie Pierre. Paris, 1931.

Epstein, Jacob
Black, Robert. *The Art of Jacob Epstein*. World Publishing Company. Cleveland, Ohio, 1942.
........Epstein, Jacob. *Let There Be Sculpture*. G. P. Putnam Sons. New York, 1940.
........Epstein, Jacob. *The Sculptor Speaks*. Doubleday Doran Company. New York, 1932.
........Powell, L. London, 1932.
........Van Dieren, Bernard. London, 1920.

Flannagan, John B.
Miller, Dorothy C., Editor. *The Sculptures of John B. Flannagan*. The Museum of Modern Art. New York, 1942.
........Valentiner, W. R. *The Letters of John B. Flannagan*. New York, 1942.
........Zigrosser, Carl, Introduction. *A Statement by the Artist*. The Museum of Modern Art. New York, 1942.

French, Daniel Chester
Adams, Adeline. Houghton Mifflin, Company. New York, 1932.
........W. W. Norton Company. New York, 1947.

Frishmuth, Harriet
Illustrated Pamphlet. Brookgreen Gardens, Georgetown, South Carolina.

Gabo, Naum
Read, Herbert. *Gabo and Pevsner*. The Museum of Modern Art. New York, 1948.

Garbe, Herbert
Herbert Garbe et La Sculpture Allemande. Editions "La Zone." Paris.

Gargallo, Pablo
    Courthion, Pierre. Paris.

Gaudier-Brzeska, Henri
    Ede, H. S. *The Savage Messiah*. Alfred A. Knopf. New York, 1931.
    ....Pound, Ezra. London.

Giacometti, Alberto
    Sartre, Jean Paul. Catalog Exhibition, Pierre Matisse Gellery. New York, 1948.

Gill, Eric
    Contemporary British Artists Series. London, 1927.
    ....Autobiography. London, 1940.

Haller, Hermann
    Kuhn, Alfred. *Der Bildhauer Hermann Haller*. Zurich, 1927.

Hazeltine, Herbert
    W. W. Norton Company. New York, 1948.

Hepworth, Barbara
    Abstraction — Creation. Paris, 1933-34.
    ....Gibson, William. London, 1946.

Hoffman, Malvina
    Alexandre, Arsène. Paris, 1930.
    Hoffman, Malvina. *Heads and Tales*. Garden City, New York, 1936.
    ....W. W. Norton Company. New York, 1948.

Huntington, Anna Hyatt
    Illustrated Pamphlet. Brookgreen Gardens, Georgetown, South Carolina.
    ....W. W. Norton Company. New York, 1947.

Kalish, Max
    Genauer, Emily, Introduction. *Max Kalish, Labor Sculpture*. New York, 1938.
    ....Lewis, N. *The Sculpture of Max Kalish*. Fine Arts Publishing Company. Cleveland, Ohio, 1933.

Kasper, Ludwig.
    Haftmann, Werner. Berlin, 1939.

Kolbe, Georg
    Binding, Rudolf G. Berlin, 1933.
    ....Justi, Ludwig. Berlin, 1931.
    ....Valentiner, Wilhelm. Munich, 1922.

Kroner, Kurt
    Grautoff, Otto. Berlin, 1927.

Lachaise, Gaston
    Gallatin, A. E. E. P. Dutton and Company. New York, 1924.
    ....Kirstein, Lincoln. Catalog of Exhibition. M. Knoedler Company. New York, 1947.

Laurens, Henri
    Le Point. Paris, 1946.

Laurent, Robert
    Portfolio. The Arts Publishing Company. Cleveland, Ohio.

Lehmbruck, Wilhelm
    Abbott, Jere. *Wilhelm Lehmbruck and Aristide Maillol*. The Museum of Modern Art. New York.
    ....Hoff, August. Berlin, 1933.
    ....Westheim, Paul. Potsdam, 1919.

Lipchitz, Jacques
    Raynal, Maurice. Paris, 1948.
    ....*Twelve Bronzes by Jacques Lipchitz*. Curt Valentin. New York, 1943.
    ....Vitrac, Roger. Paris, 1929.
    ....Waldemar, George. Paris.

Maillol, Aristide
    Abbott, Jere. *Wilhelm Lehmbruck and Aristide Maillol*. The Museum of Modern Art, New York.
    ....Cosmo, Pierre. Paris, 1926
    ....Dénis, Maurice. Paris, 1925.
    ....Librairie Gallimard. Paris, 1926.
    ....René-Jean. Editions Braun. Paris.
    ....Rewald, John. Paris, 1939.

Manship, Paul
    Illustrated Pamphlet. Brookgreen Gardens, Georgetown, South Carolina.
    ....Vitry, Paul. Paris, 1927.
    ....W. W. Norton Company. New York, 1947.

Marini, Marino
    Contini, Gianfranco. *Vingt Scultures de Marino Marini*. Lugano, 1944.
    ....Editione U. Firenze, 1946.

Mascherini, Marcello
    Pica, Agnodomenier. Milano, 1945.

Matisse, Henri
    Barr, Alfred H., Jr. The Museum of Modern Art. New York, 1931.
    ....Guéguen, Pierre. *The Sculpture of Henri Matisse*. Paris, 1938.

Mestrovic, Ivan
    Brinton, Christian. Catalog of Exhibition. Brooklyn Museum, 1924.
    ....Syracuse University Press. (In preparation)

Milles, Carl
    Rogers, Meyric R. Yale University Press, 1940.

Modigliani, Amedeo
    Dale, Maud. New York, 1929.
    ....Franchi Raffaello. Firenze, 1946.
    ....Salmon, André. Paris, 1926.

Moholy-Nagy, László
 Konstruktionen Portfolio. Hanover, 1925.
Moore, Henry
 Read, Herbert. London, 1934.
 ....Read, Herbert. Introductory Statement by the Artist. *The Sculptures and Drawings of Henry Moore.* Curt Valentin. New York, 1944.
 ....Sweeney, James Johnson. New York, 1946.
Nadelman, Elie
 Kirstein, Lincoln. The Museum of Modern Art. New York, 1948.
Nicholson, Ben
 Abstraction-Creation. Paris, 1933-34.
 ....An Album of Photographs Published by the Artist. London, 1940.
Orloff, Chana
 Nouvelle Revue Française. Paris, 1927.
 ....Werth, Léon. Paris.
Pevsner, Antoine
 Read, Herbert. *Gabo and Pevsner.* The Museum of Modern Art. New York, 1948.
Picasso, Pablo
 Barr, Alfred H., Jr. *Fifty Years of His Art.* New York, 1946.
Piccirilli, Attilio
 Lombardo, Josef Vincent. Pitman Publishing Company. New York, 1944.
Pompon
 Brielle, Roger. Paris.
Putnam, Brenda
 Illustrated Pamphlet. Brookgreen Gardens, Georgetown, South Carolina.
 ....W. W. Norton Company. New York, 1948.
Raedecker, John
 Bremmer, H. P. De Spieghel. Amsterdam.
Renoir, Pierre-Auguste
 Haesaerts, Paul. *Renoir, Sculptor.* New York, 1947.
Rimmer, William
 Bartlett, Truman H. *The Life of William Rimmer.* Boston, 1882.
 ....Kirstein, Lincoln. Catalog of Exhibition. Whitney Museum of American Art. New York, 1940.
Rodin, Auguste
 Cladel, J. *Auguste Rodin, L'Oeuvre et L'Homme.* Paris, 1908.
 ....Kahn, G. Paris, 1909.
 ....Rilke, Rainer Maria. Leipzig, 1913. (English translation by Jessie Lemont and Hans Trausilo. Fine Editions Press. New York, 1945.)
 ....*Sculptures de Rodin.* Editions "Tel." Paris.

Rogers, John
 Groups of Statuary. New York, 1890.
Saint-Gaudens, Augustus
 Catalog of Memorial Exhibition. Metropolitan Museum of Art. New York, 1908.
 ....Cortissoz, Royal. New York, 1907.
 ....Hind, C. L. New York, 1908.
 ....*Reminiscences* — Edited by Homer Saint-Gaudens. 2 vols. Century Company. New York, 1913.
 ....W. W. Norton Company. New York, 1948.
Scheibe, Richard
 Kroll, Bruno. Introduction, Georg Kolbe. Berlin, 1939.
Schlemmer, Oskar
 Schmidt, Paul F. *Jahrbuch der Junger Kunst.* Leipzig, 1921.
Sintenis, Renée.
 Crevel, René. Berlin, 1930.
Smith, David
 Blake, William and Stead, Christina. *Medals for Dishonor.* Catalog of Exhibition. Willard Gallery. New York, 1940.
Vantongerloo, Georges
 De Sikkel. *L'Art et Son Avenir.* Santpoort, 1924.
Waugh, Sidney
 Catalog of an Exhibition of Designs for Glass by Twenty-Seven Contemporary Artists. Steuben Glass Company. New York, 1940.
 ....The Steuben Glass Company. New York, 1939.
 ....W. W. Norton Company. New York, 1948.
Weinman, Adolph
 Illustrated Pamphlet. Brookgreen Gardens, Georgetown, South Carolina.
Whitney, Gertrude Vanderbilt
 Catalog of Memorial Exhibition. Whitney Museum of American Art. New York, 1943.
Williams, Wheeler
 Illustrated Pamphlet. Brookgreen Gardens, Georgetown, South Carolina.
 ....W. W. Norton Company. New York, 1947.
Zadkine, Ossip
 Raynal, Maurice. Rome, 1924.
Zorach, William
 American Artists Group. New York, 1945.
 ....Wingert, Paul S. *The Sculpture of William Zorach.* New York, 1938.

SURVEYS AND CATALOGS OF
EXHIBITIONS AND COLLECTIONS

Almanach Neuer Kunst in der Schweiz. Allianz. Zurich, 1940.

American Art Today. New York World's Fair. New York, 1939.

American Sculptors. Twentieth Century Index of American Artists. College Art Association, New York, 1933-37.

American Sources of Modern Art. The Museum of Modern Art. New York, 1933.

Americans, 1942. Miller, Dorothy C., Editor. Eighteen Artists from Nine States. The Museum of Modern Art. New York, 1942.

Art. Hors-Série De L'Architecture D'Aujourd'-hui. Paris.

Art in America in Modern Times. Cahill, Holger and Barr, Alfred H., Jr. New York, 1934.

Art Italien Moderne. Scheiwiller, Giovani. Paris, 1930.

Art of This Century. Catalog Collection Peggy Guggenheim. Editor, Peggy Guggenheim. New York, 1942.

Arte Italiana Del Nostro Tempo. Cairola, Stefano. Bergamo, 1946.

Arte Russe Moderne. Salmon, André. Paris, 1928.

Artists for Victory. An Exhibition of Contemporary American Art. Metropolitan Museum of Art. New York, 1942.

Arts of Painting and Sculpture, The. Fry, Roger. London, 1932.

British Sculpture. Newton, Eric. London, 1947.

Brookgreen Gardens Sculpture. Proske, Beatrice Gilman. Georgetown, South Carolina.

Catalog of the Collection. Whitney Museum of American Art. New York, 1931.

Circle. International Survey of Constructive Art. London, 1937.

Contemporary American Sculpture. Catalog of the Exhibition of the National Sculpture Society. New York, 1923.

Contemporary American Sculpture. Catalog of the Exhibition of the National Sculpture Society of San Francisco. New York, 1929.

Deutsche Bildhauer Der Gegenwart. Hentzen, Alfred. Berlin, 1934.

Die Kunst Des xx Jahrhunderts. Einstein, Carl. Berlin.

Fourteen Americans. Miller, Dorothy C., Editor. The Museum of Modern Art. New York, 1946.

German Painting and Sculpture. Barr, Alfred H., Jr. New York, 1931.

Handbook of Modern French Sculpture. Eaton, D. C. Paris, 1913.

Konstruktivisten. Schmidt, George. Catalog Exhibition Kunsthalle. Basel, 1937.

La Sculpture Française Contemporaine. Letourneur, René. Monaco, 1944.

La Sculpture Moderne en France. Basler, Adolphe. Paris, 1928.

Modern Art in America. Cheney, Martha Chandler. New York and London, 1939.

Modern English Art. Blake, Christopher. London, 1937.

Modern European Art. Collings, E. H. R. London, 1929.

Modern Plastic (English Edition). Giedion-Welcker. Zurich, 1946.

Modern Russian Art. Lozowick, Louis. Société Anonyme. New York, 1925.

Modern Sculpture. Hudnut, Joseph. New York, 1929.

Moderne Plastik. Radenberg, W. 1912.

Museum in Action, A. Catalog of an Exhibition of American Paintings and Sculptures from the Museum Collection. Essay, Holger Cahill. Newark Museum, Newark, New Jersey, 1944.

Museum of Living Art. Gallatin, A. E. Collection. New York, 1937.

Neue Kunst in Russland, 1914-1919. Umanskij, Konstantin. Potsdam, Munich, 1920.

New Architectural Sculpture, The. Agard, Walter R. London, 1935.

Notas Sobre La Pintura y La Escultura en Venezuela. Nucete-Sardi, José. Caracas, 1940.

Nueve Artistas Colombianos. Zalamea, Georg. Bogota, 1941.

Painters and Sculptors of Modern America. Wheeler, Monroe. New York, 1942.

Paintings and Sculpture by Living Americans. Barr, Alfred H., Jr. 1931.

Painting and Sculpture in the Museum of Modern Art. Barr, Alfred H., Jr. New York, 1942.

Sculpteurs D'Aujourd'Hui. Fierens, Paul. Paris, 1933.

Sculptors Guild, The. Catalogs: 1938, 1939, 1941, New York; 1941-42, Travelling Exhibition; 1942, 1948, New York.

Sculpture of the Western Hemisphere. Collection of International Business Machines Corporation. New York, 1942. Includes work of: American Sculptors; Canadian Sculptors; Latin American Sculptors.

Sculpture Today in Great Britain. Broadbent, Arthur J. London, 1944.

Scultura Italiana Contemporanea. Borgellini, Pierre. Firenze, 1945.

Scultura Vivente. Bragaglio, A. G. Milano, 1928.

Some Modern Sculptors. Casson, Stanley. London, 1928.

Twentieth Century American Sculpture. Cahill, Holger. Catalog of the Collection of the Newark Museum. Newark, New Jersey, 1945.

Twentieth Century Sculptors. Casson, Stanley. London, 1930.

Twentieth Century Sculpture. Catalog of Exhibition at Albright Art Gallery. Buffalo, 1927.

Twentieth Century Sculpture. Catalog of the Collection of the Art Institute of Chicago. 1940.

Twentieth Century Sculpture. Coquiot, Gustave. Paris, 1914.

Twentieth Century Sculpture. Guéguen, Pierre. Paris, 1945.

United American Sculptors. Catalog of Exhibition. New York, 1939.

XX Siecle Sculpture. Paris, 1939.

CONTEMPORARY ESTHETICS

Aesthetics, Ethics and History in the Visual Arts. Berenson, Bernard. Pantheon Books. New York, 1948.

Art and Geometry. Irvings, William M., Jr. Harvard University Press, 1946.

Art and Society. Read, Herbert. London, 1945.

Art Now. Read, Herbert. New York and London, 1936.

Constructivist Manifesto, The. Gabo, Naum, and Pevsner, Antoine. Moscow, 1920. (Abridged French translation, *Abstraction - Creation.* Paris, 1932.)

Cubism and Abstract Art. Barr, Alfred H., Jr. The Museum of Modern Art. New York, 1936.

Cubismo, Futurismo, Expressionismo. Pavollini, Corrado. Bologna, 1926.

Cubists and Post Impressionism. Eddy, Arthur, Jerome. Chicago, 1919.

De L'Impressionisme en Sculpture. Claris, E. Paris, 1903.

Der Geist der Kubismus and Die Künste. Bluemmer, Rudolf. *Der Sturm.* Berlin.

Education Through Art. Read, Herbert. London, 1944.

Entwicklungsgeschichte der Modernen Kunst. Meier-Graefe, Julius. Munich, 1914.

Estetica e Arte Futurista. Boccioni, Umberto. Milano, 1914.

Expressionism in Art. Cheney, Sheldon. New York, 1934.

Foundations of Aesthetics, The. Richards, J. K., Ogden, C. K., and Wood, James. Lear Publishers. New York, 1948.

Government and the Arts. Overmyer, Grace. New York, 1939.

Grass Roots of Art, The. Read, Herbert. New York, 1947.

Isms of Art, The. Lissitzky, El and Arp, Hans. Leipzig, 1925.

Language of Vision. Kepes, Gyorgy. Chicago, 1947.

Last Lectures. *Fry, Roger*. New York and Cambridge, 1939.

Mathematical Basis of The Arts, The. Schillinger, Joseph. New York.

Meaning of Modern Sculpture, The. Wilenski, R. H. London.

Modern Movements in Art. Wilenski, R. H. New York, 1926.

New Vision, The. Moholy-Nagy, László. New York, 1946.

Origins of Modern Sculpture. Valentiner, W. R. New York, 1946.

Pittura, Scultura, Futuriste, Dinamismo Plastico. Boccioni, Umberto. Milano, 1914.

Primer of Modern Art, A. Cheney, Sheldon. Tudor Publishing Company. New York, 1945.

Problems of the Sculptor. Adriani, Bruno. New York, 1943.

Scultura Futurista. Boccioni, Umberto. Firenze, 1914.

Vision and Design. Fry, Roger. New York, 1947 (New Edition).

Vision in Motion. Moholy-Nagy, L. Chicago, 1947.

What Are Masterpieces? Stein, Gertrude. Los Angeles, 1940.

EARLY AMERICAN SCULPTURE

American Figureheads and Their Carvers. Pinkney, Pauline A. New York, 1940.

American Folk Sculpture. Cahill, Holger. Newark Museum. Newark, New Jersey, 1931.

American Masters of Sculpture. Caffin, Charles, H. New York, 1913.

American Painting and Sculpture. 1862-1932. Cahill, Holger. The Museum of Modern Art. New York, 1932.

American Painting and Sculpture of the 18th, 19th, *and* 20th *Centuries*. Hitchcock, Henry-Russel, Jr. Wadsworth Atheneum. Hartford, Connecticut, 1935.

Art of the Exposition, The. Neuhaus, Eugen. The Galleries of the Panama Pacific Exposition. San Francisco, 1915.

Catalog of the Palmer Marbles. Church of the Divine Unity. New York and Albany, 1836.

Dictionary of American Painters, Sculptors, and Engravers. Fielding, Mantle. Philadelphia, 1926.

Directory 19th *Century Sculptors*. Clement, Clara Erskine. New York, 1907.

Exhibition of American Sculpture, An. Metropolitan Museum of Art. New York, 1918.

Famous Sculptors of America. McSpadden, J. Walker. New York, 1923.

Fry, Erwin. Adams, Philip. *The Sculpture of Erwin Fry*. Ohio State University Press, 1939.

History and Ideals of American Art, The. Neuhaus, Eugen. Stanford University Press, 1931.

History of American Sculpture, The. Taft, Lorado. New York, 1903.

Rogers, John. Smith, Chetwood and M. *Thought and Wrought by John Rogers*. Boston, 1934.

Rush, William. Marceau, Henri. *The First Native Sculptor*. Philadelphia, 1937.

Sculpture of the Exposition Palaces and Courts. James, Juliet. San Francisco. Panama Pacific Exposition.

Spirit of American Sculpture, The. Adams, Adeline. New York, 1929.

Yankee Stonecutters. The First American School of Sculpture. Gardner, Albert Teneyck. New York, 1945.

THE TECHNIQUE OF SCULPTURE

Materials and Methods of Sculpture, The. Rich, Jack. New York, 1947.

Metal Casting of Sculpture. Clarke, Carl Dame. The Standard Arts Press. Baltimore, Maryland.

Modelling and Sculpture. Toft, Albert. Lippincott. Philadelphia, 1929.

Modern Sculpture, Its Methods and Ideals. Maryan, Herbert. London, 1933.

Molding and Casting. Its Technic and Application. Clarke, Carl Dame. Baltimore, 1938.

Primer for Chiselers, A. Rood, John. Stanford University Press, 1948.

Sculpture Inside and Out. Hoffman, Malvina. New York, 1939.

Wood Sculpture. Rood, John. Athens, Ohio, 1940.

Zorach Explains Sculpture. What It Means and How It Is Made. Zorach, William. New York, 1947.